GEORGE VERWER

more drops

MYSTERY
MERCY
MESSIOLOGY

CWR

'I love George Verwer and I love this book! Few people on earth are better placed to speak provocatively into the life of a church than George who for decades has circumnavigated the globe and relentlessly gone after the least, last and lost. Along the way, with God's help, he's produced the most remarkable movement that is day in, day out, seeing multiple thousands of people touched by the gospel.'
Andy Hawthorne OBE is a British evangelist, author and founder of The Message Trust.

'Verwer has, for over 50 years, been a grace-oriented reconciler, a friend of sinners, and a lighthouse of practical wisdom. This book is just that – not a thriller, nor a devotional, but a handbook of applied biblical insights of experience which may help the reader avoid getting wrecked on the shoals of life.'
Dr Greg Livingstone (Founder of Frontiers)

'This is vintage Verwer! In this book, one of the finest modern preachers captures the simplicity and passion which studs his spoken ministry as he touches on issues of great consequence for the Christian Church. This slender, readable book is a classic in practical theology and discipleship. Its contents are not so much drops gained from a dripping tap but gems gleaned from a transparent man. I aim to put a copy of this book into the hands of all my students.'
Rev Dr Tony Sargent (Principal Emeritus of the International Christian College)

'In filming, travelling and working with George I have been truly blessed by the 'drops of Living Water' that he shares every day, not just in the interviews, but in the way he leads his life. I have been privileged, but the reader too will be blessed, inspired, encouraged and capture some of the passion of George – that the world might know and that we become more like Jesus.'
Malcolm Turner (Executive Director, Christian Television Association)

'This is George Verwer at his best! Each chapter stands alone and you will find priceless nuggets of truth in each one. I think the word 'Messiology' will be in common use before long.'
Peter Maiden (former director of the Keswick Convention, International Director Emeritus of OM)

'This is an inspired book and is a MUST to read! Its heights, depths and breadth will give us, the reader, a mirror by which to be examined in our spiritual walk. The challenges are a testimony from George as to how our God, through Scripture and fellow travellers, has influenced, strengthened and spurred him on and, I am convinced, will touch every part of our own spiritual journey.'
Robin Oake (former Chief Constable and author of *Father Forgive: The Forgotten 'F' Word*)

'I so enjoyed making my way through the short, punchy chapters. There is humour in this book and a heart cry for reality, humility and balance.'
Michael Wiltshire (former journalist for *The Financial Times*)

Copyright © George Verwer 2015

Published 2015 by CWR, Waverley Abbey House, Waverley Lane, Farnham, Surrey, GU9 8EP, UK. Registered Charity No. 294387. Registered Limited Company No. 1990308.

The right of George Verwer to be identified as the author of this work has been asserted by him in accordance with the Copyright, Designs and Patents Act 1988, sections 77 and 78.

For a list of National Distributors visit www.cwr.org.uk/distributors

Unless otherwise indicated, all Scripture references are from the Holy Bible, New International Version Anglicised (NIV) Copyright © 1979, 1984, 2011 by Biblica (formerly International Bible Society). Used by permission of Hodder & Stoughton Publishers, a Hachette UK company. All rights reserved. 'NIV' is a registered trademark of Biblica (formerly International Bible Society). UK trademark number 1448790. Other Scripture quotations are marked AV and are taken from the Authorised Version, reproduced in accordance with Cambridge University Press permission request guidelines.

Concept development, editing, design and production by CWR.

Printed in the UK by the Linney Group.

ISBN: 978-1-78259-487-1

Dedication

This book is dedicated to all the people I have met, through OM or otherwise, for whom, humanly speaking, life has not worked out well. These people are not on plan A or plan B, but more like plan M. When I speak with them, I remind them of God's big alphabet and urge them to embrace radical grace and press on.

I am reminded again and again of 1 John 3:16 – 'This is how we know what love is: Jesus Christ laid down his life for us. And we ought to lay down our lives for our brothers and sisters.'

Acknowledgements

I want to thank all those who helped make this book a reality. In particular, I want to acknowledge the hundreds of people who have had a major spiritual input (sometimes via tapes or books) in my life. Firstly my spiritual father, Billy Graham, and my second most influential Christian leader, Dr Oswald J. Smith. I also want to especially thank the Lord for my sister Barbara, my parents, my wife Drena and all my family.

Contents

Foreword

More Drops: Mystery, Mercy and Messiology is an important book for two reasons: firstly, the author, and secondly, the message.

First, George Verwer is the founder of Operation Mobilisation (OM), which, under God, has been one of the most globally significant mission agencies in the twentieth century. Beginning in the late 1950s, OM is well-known for:

- Its strong commitment to both the publication and distribution of Christian literature of enduring worth and evangelistic impact in many languages and countries across the globe. OM strongly backed the publication of the first edition of *Operation World*, a great resource for mission-minded Christians.
- OM was probably the first mission agency in the world to emphasise and create opportunities for short-term mission service (even though they still give prominence to life-long service). As a result, many leaders from other agencies such as YWAM, IFES and Frontiers have spent time with OM.
- Under George, OM also developed the Ship Ministries of *Logos*, *Doulos* and *Logos Hope* which have been a means of bringing the gospel to millions.
- When it was unfashionable to do so, from the 1960s onwards, OM focussed on taking the gospel to gospel-resistant cultures such as India (and the Indian sub-continent), Turkey, Eastern Europe and the Middle East – all of these ministries are increasingly bearing fruit today.

- Many other mission agencies have been started by people who were shaped by OM, perhaps most notably the Good Shepherd Movement among the Dalits in India, and Pioneers, focusing especially on unreached people groups and major cities.

Because of these creative and strategic innovations, many (including myself) would regard George Verwer as being perhaps the most significant missionary leader and statesman to come out of North America in the last 60 years. With that track record, if you ask me, anything he writes is worth reading!

Secondly, there is the message. This book summarises convictions that have undergirded both George and OM's ministry for almost 60 years, such as:

- The foundational need to be solidly rooted in the truths of the Bible, while exercising grace towards those who hold different opinions.
- The call to radical discipleship in serving Christ, including a disciplined, joyful and godly lifestyle.
- Believing the best about other Christians, eschewing gossip, the importance of the avoidance of cherishing resentment and bitterness to those who may have harmed us, and a generosity of spirit in partnering with others.
- Trusting that in His mysterious and providential sovereignty, God may choose to bring much blessing, even out of many very messy situations (what George calls 'messiology').
- The importance of balancing the bold proclamation of the gospel alongside ministries of compassion.
- The ongoing urgency of reaching the lost or the unreached. This is still George and OM's heartbeat today.

These are the convictions that have strengthened and driven George's ministry for decades – and they are worth hearing.

In the last chapter of *More Drops*, George says that 'if the message of mystery, mercy, Messiology (and grace) has not come out in this book then I have failed'. He has not failed. And because of that, these confessions of a lifelong learner and mission leader are well worth reading. If digested and applied, this book could make radical (and whole) disciples of many in this next generation.

Lindsay Brown
(International Director of the Lausanne Movement for World Evangelisation, 2008–Present; General Secretary of the International Fellowship of Evangelical Students (IFES), 1991–2007; ex-OMer, 1976–1977)

Introduction

Mystery, Mercy, Messiology

For some years I have been praying and struggling about writing another book. I do not see myself as a gifted writer and do not find much time to give myself to it and that makes it even harder to press on in the task.

My passion in regard to books, which goes back to my very conversion, has always been other people's books. I have spent a lifetime publishing and distributing books by great Christian authors, both men and women. Even as I look back at my books I think one of the best features is the way I introduce my readers to so many other books. If you have some of my other books why not check this out? There is a list of my other titles and those that I recommend written by other authors, at the end of this book.

I stand amazed that over a million copies of my own books have now gone out around the world in about fifty different languages. One of the first books, *Hunger for Reality* (Authentic Lifestyle, 1996 – originally entitled *Come! Live! Die!*) has brought me over 25,000 personal letters. Wherever I go, I have people tell me how these books have helped them. It's been a great encouragement and I can only give thanks to the Lord.

In my earlier book, *Drops from a Leaking Tap* (Authentic Media, 2011), only one chapter tries to set forth the biggest change in my life and the history of Operation Mobilisation (OM): the embracing of social concern and social action as a vital part of our ministry. In this latest book, *More Drops:*

Mystery, Mercy and Messiology, I want to elaborate more on that and what I have learned in the past years about the challenge and complexity of this and how easy it is to get into difficulty.

I don't know how to put it, but I feel that many leaders and Christians in general are making big mistakes in their lives and ministry. Since I have made some myself, I hope my sharing can help some to avoid pitfalls. I have learned from observation that in some difficulties there is no way out without serious damage to oneself and the body of Christ. As you will read about in Chapter 1, when I was about 18 years of age, whilst still in the fire extinguisher business, I headed west to the Grand Canyon, reading the book of Acts. This led me to what I made at that time my life verse:

> *'However, I consider my life worth nothing to me;*
> *my only aim is to finish the race and complete the*
> *task the Lord Jesus has given me – the task of*
> *testifying to the good news of God's grace'.*
>
> **(Acts 20:24)**

Now, looking back on 58 years in Christ, I can say that this has since happened more or less on a daily basis. My prayer, in whatever years remain, is that it will continue to be a reality. Can you feel the reality and passion of this verse? Can you read it and also make it your goal and aim in life? If so, then I think you will find this book helpful in more ways than one.

As in *Drops from a Leaking Tap*, each chapter in *More Drops* can stand on its own. Due to my memory, there may be a slight overlap with some things written in other books, although reading something that is vital and important twice will not harm us.

To be honest, my prayer is that *More Drops* will also give people a desire to read or re-read my other books that will be listed at the end of this book; in many places they are available free of charge. It's also my prayer that others will join us in getting these messages out. I have a great passion to pass on to the next generation as much as possible from all that I have learned from the Lord and His people. In some ways, my writing to some may seem a bit 'out of the box', but on the other hand it is very basic and not that hard to understand, especially if people have both some common sense and spiritual discernment.

As I finish typing this introduction, I am listening to some great classical piano music by Tchaikovsky, Mozart and Beethoven. A few days ago I took Drena, my wife, to a great concert at the Royal Albert Hall in London. It is my prayer that at least some of what I write, especially about forgiveness and grace, will be music to your spiritual ears and that your life, as a result of reading this book, will become more of a symphony than it may be at this present time. I will try to bring into reality and balance the challenge of radical discipleship expressed in books like *Radical* (Random House, 2010) by David Platt and *The Grace Awakening* (Thomas Nelson, 2006) by Charles Swindoll. I want to add to it the plea for global mission and evangelism at any cost, that all the people of the world might have the gospel and that there be a Church among all peoples. I am hoping that some who read this book will join me in this great vision and task. I answer every email personally, so do give it a try at **george.verwer@om.org**

In His grace and grip,

George Verwer

CHAPTER 1

Messiology

When I first wrote *Out of the Comfort Zone* (Bethany House, 2000), one of my greatest burdens was to see more of a grace-awakening, especially among those involved in global missions. In fact, the chapter on 'Grace' was combined with the chapter on 'Leadership' to become a standalone booklet called 'Grace Awakened Leadership' that we give away. Again and again, we hear of tensions among those working to reach the world with the gospel and many local churches seem to go through very heavy and complex divisions. To be honest, although we hear of many breakthroughs in relationships, in some situations things in this area seem to be worse than ever before.

I believe what I have written in the past has failed to share my theology of 'Messiology' adequately and I want to try to do that now. Messiology is my own term, but it's actually all about God and how He works and has been working for thousands of years.

The Bible is full of teaching and exhortation about living a godly life of reality and integrity. If we follow 1 Corinthians 13, it will totally change our lives and our churches. I also shared this in one of my earlier books, *The Revolution of Love* (Authentic Media, 2008).

> *If I speak in the tongues of men or of angels, but do not have love, I am only a resounding gong or a clanging cymbal. If I have the gift of prophecy and can fathom all mysteries and all knowledge, and if I have a faith that can move mountains, but do not have love, I am nothing. If I give all I possess to the poor and give over my body to hardship that I may boast, but do not have love, I gain nothing.*
>
> (1 Cor. 13:1–3)

We also see God working through all kinds of what I call 'messy situations' which is where I got my term Messiology. For years I have quoted my own proverb, 'Where two or three are gathered together in His Name, sooner or later there will be a mess'. Almost always the congregation laughs. I then ask, how many have experienced that and most hands go up. I then go on to explain Messiology. It is simply that God, in His patience, mercy and passion to bring men and women to Himself, often does great things in the midst of a mess. That is not an excuse to sin, fail or to make a mess, every Christian should want to do the opposite, but it's the other side of the coin. It's God's way of working. Large portions of Acts and the majority of the epistles demonstrate this.

Gordon MacDonald's book, *Rebuilding Your Broken World* (Thomas Nelson, 2004), together with many other great books, has helped me develop this conviction or belief and it is now very strong in my heart. It has helped me understand God and His work more than almost anything else. I sometimes refer to this as 'radical grace'.

In fifty-seven years, in over ninety countries, in thousands of churches and other organisations, I have often observed some kind of mess. Sometimes clear sin is involved that needs to be repented of. Other times it is just silly, or however you want to describe nonsensical behaviour on the part of God's children. I have said, and I feel it strongly, that no matter how filled we are with the Holy Spirit, we are still very human. Our humanness has its beautiful side, as well as its messy side.

I admire many Christian leaders, and try to have a grace-awakened attitude toward all of them, but in all these fifty-seven years I have seen Christian leaders, including missionaries, do some of the most ridiculous things and say even more ridiculous things … and sometimes it can be me. Yet, as I have observed more carefully, I have seen God working in the midst of it. You will probably not want to read this, but I have seen many people used by God who were clearly living in sin at the same time. We have seen pastors being used by God, seeing people saved, seeing the church grow and people being discipled and yet discovered later they were in regular adultery and unfaithfulness. I am speaking of married people with children. Of course often, after time, it catches up with them, they are fired, sometimes get divorced or worse. Years later you meet the person with their new spouse and discover he/she is being used in ministry. If I wrote a whole book on this I could give hundreds of similar examples. How do we explain it? MESSIOLOGY!

Some other key words surrounding this idea are 'mystery' and 'mercy'. The last verses of Romans 11 have helped me again and again: 'Oh, the depth of the riches of the wisdom and knowledge of God! How unsearchable his judgments, and his paths beyond tracing out!' (Rom. 11:33).

The hardest thing for some people, especially leaders to accept, is when God is working in a mighty way through someone they think has wrong theology. How can this be? I meet people who are upset with some of the television speakers/evangelists and others in that unique complex world. Many people tell me that they will not even watch it. Whole articles have been written against certain Christian television and I find myself agreeing with some of what they say. Things I have seen and heard on these programmes could make me weep, especially the extreme fund-raising tricks of the so-called trade. But, do not be surprised when you get to heaven and meet hundreds of thousands who came to Christ through some of these ministries! Do we need more of the Apostle Paul's attitude as shown in Philippians 1:15–18?

> It is true that some preach Christ out of envy and rivalry, but others out of goodwill. The latter do so out of love, knowing that I am put here for the defence of the gospel. The former preach Christ out of selfish ambition, not sincerely, supposing that they can stir up trouble for me while I am in chains. But what does it matter? The important thing is that in every way, whether from false motives or true, Christ is preached. And because of this I rejoice.

It is clear and hard to accept that God uses ministries and people that we may want nothing to do with. He seems to support ministries that I would not send even £5 to. We want to explain these things and try to fit them in our box, but sometimes we find they will not fit! The answer – Messiology! I need a whole other book to explain this in detail. I have two writers who want to help me write it, but I doubt it will be done. It would be all too messy!

Another vital, key area where things get very messy is in the whole area of finance and sending funds to mission fields for people and projects. With horror stories we can 'prove' anything we want, so people tell horror stories of the misuse of funds on the field and it scares people from sending any money at all. A hot word is the word 'dependency' and some very extreme books and articles have been written about this. I believe this brings a lot of confusion. I am convinced that history will show that generosity and taking the risk of supporting a project (like a school) even thousands of miles away, have been major positive factors in taking the gospel forward and establishing His Church. I wish I had the time and gifting to write a whole book about this too.

It is a sad fact that some people will not support a new school or other similar projects if they do not see how it can be self-supporting right away. This is a huge mistake especially in places like India. Self-supporting schools have been the emphasis in India for many years and that is why there are very few good schools for the extreme poor (generally Dalits or tribal people), whereas there are thousands of schools among those who can pay (I am not saying this is wrong though). In the complex situation of extreme poverty, we must expect to put a lot of money in before a school can sustain itself. It may be a couple of decades, when people who graduate from these schools have jobs, before things can change. Can people even imagine what we are up against in India with almost 300 million locked into the extreme poverty of untouchability? These special situations, and there are many around the world, need hyper-special generosity. Throwing up the 'dependency' scare tactic can be one of the great hindrances. That doesn't mean we should not exercise discernment and research in connection with all that we give. Having the right people on the field to handle the finance and the projects is the most important factor of all. However, even with some things going wrong and messy situations, I still believe history will show that God was doing way more in the midst of this mess than we realised at the time. People, churches or foundations who think that they wasted money on a project that went totally wrong may discover many great results of their giving when they get to heaven.

In all of this we need to have more wisdom and common sense and especially be aware of what I call 'destructive idealism'. If this idealism combines with the kind of perfectionist streak that many of us have, it causes a lot of discouragement, disunity and confusion. That is why there are so many books setting forth someone's teaching or agenda, which give an inaccurate picture of other people, churches and organisations and what they are doing. A little more wisdom, patience and humility would go a long way in taking us into greater reality and victory.

As I finish this chapter, controversy is going on among missions and church leaders, more than I have known in my lifetime. There is a large group of people who want to be considered biblical and evangelical and yet who seem to, in a very subtle way, deny the very basics of the faith, like the lostness of all who are outside of Christ and the substitutionary death of Christ and many other basic doctrines that most evangelical leaders and agencies have subscribed to for hundreds of years.

I find that many books are so critical of the Church and of the present evangelical global movement which now involves hundreds of millions of people in almost every nation of the world. It seems like they are saying that Hudson Taylor, John Stott, Billy Graham, John Calvin, Watchman Nee, Bakht Singh, William Carey, Dr Francis Schaeffer, Charles Spurgeon, D.L. Moody, Festo Kivengere, William Booth, John Wesley, Amy Carmichael, Augustine of Hippo and hundreds of others who have helped this movement become what it is today had it all wrong. They might not verbally say it exactly, but, to me, that's what their writing clearly implies. Their books that have become so popular, do have many good things to say, but, in my opinion, again and again, they also move from truth to error leaving the readers in doubt and confusion, which has created a great disunity in the Body of Christ and caused quite a few churches to split. Often, the natural result is criticism of their own church or denomination. This can of course cause many to leave their church and start new churches often based more on reaction than biblical truth. For me, it's leading to a higher level of Messiology than ever. I believe that in the midst of it we need more wisdom, love and discernment than ever before. We need the reality of pressing on 'with our eyes on Jesus' in the centre of the difficulties and challenges.

CHAPTER 2

Fire Extinguishers, Books and Proverbs

As I am writing this, it is our daughter Christa's birthday and I want to dedicate this chapter to her. One of my many failures in those early days was to not be there in the hospital in Leigh, Lancashire when she was born, luckily Drena was there! I was coming in from meetings from somewhere overseas and did not quite make the mega event. We named her after Christa Fisher, who is from what was then East Germany and who later became Mrs Ray Eicher. They were for years, along with Alfy Franks, the leaders of our work in India. Christa had come to Jesus in the early days through our ministry in Madrid where we first lived when we came to Europe in the fall of 1960. Ben, our first son, was born shortly after that.

In the summer of 1957, three of us were planning to go to Mexico to distribute literature and reach people with the gospel. I had studied Spanish both in High School and my first year of

Maryville College where I met Walter Borchard, my roommate, and Dale Rhoton who very quickly became a strong godly influence in my life. We did not go until around mid-July as Dale was studying at Wheaton Summer School and Walter and I were selling Christian books door-to-door in my home area of northeast New Jersey. I had been selling fire extinguishers in that area for a number of years and that business was going great. I would light a fire in a pan in front of someone's house while they watched me put it out with this little 'Presto Fire Extinguisher'. I soon had lots of other people selling them as I sold at a big profit, both wholesale and retail. My boss was a Jewish man, Mr Finklestein in Manhattan, and it was special for someone aged sixteen to go and meet him. He was so happy about my sales that he made me the exclusive agent for Bergen County and so I officially registered my company, Bergen County Sales Co. It was all going great until Jesus came into my life and led me into the 'Eternal Fire Extinguishers' business. During the summers of 1955, 1956 and right after my conversion it was fire extinguishers, but by 1957 it was Bibles and Christian books and soon I would be starting a mission called, 'Send the Light'.

Whilst Walter and I were in New Jersey selling Christian books door-to-door, both to get the message out and to earn money for our trip to Mexico, I remember well that there was a lady in North Haledon who bought a lot of books, which made me very happy. I think she could tell that I was big on zeal but maybe weak on wisdom and so she challenged me to read the 'wisdom' book of Proverbs in the Old Testament. I had been slowly making my way through the Old Testament, but was not sure I had gotten that far. She said something I have never forgotten, *'A Proverb a day will keep the devil away'* and then showed me in the Bible that there were 31 chapters in Proverbs, one for every day in the month. You can be sure I have been in the Proverbs ever since. Little did I know what God had ahead for me and how much the exhortations and wisdom of this book would help me in my forty-six-year pilgrimage as leader of Send the Light, which later in Europe became 'Operation Mobilisation'.

What are some of the highlights that hit me hard? Here are some of the main themes:

1. Victory over lust

There are hundreds of verses about sex in the Bible and some of them seem pretty wild and out of the box, like Proverbs 5:18–19:

> *May your fountain be blessed, and may you rejoice in the wife of your youth. A loving doe, a graceful deer – may her breasts satisfy you always, may you ever be intoxicated with her love.*

Little did I realise as a young Christian, so hungry for God and so radically committed to Jesus and His Word, that I would battle with this all my life. Before my conversion, I had gotten into it in a small way always believing it was wrong, but only at conversion did I get the strength to battle and defeat this in my life. At that time I do not think I had even seen one sort of hard porn image, but I am sure without Jesus I would have gone down that road. Again and again I would read Proverbs 5, 6 and 7 and verses like these and other similar teaching scattered throughout the Bible, and they laid a solid foundation for my life-long battle with lust.

> *All at once he followed her like an ox going to the slaughter, like a deer stepping into a noose … Many are the victims she has brought down; her slain are a mighty throng. Her house is a highway to the grave, leading down to the chambers of death.*
>
> **(Prov. 7:22,26–27)**

We never dreamed at the time that that trip to Mexico would also lead us to become one of the major distributors of the Bible and books on this subject in many languages around the world. The chapter on the subject of lust in my previous book *Drops from a Leaking Tap*, which first came out as a magazine article, is one of the hardest things I ever allowed into print.

2. Sins of the Tongue

Sins of the tongue are one of the big themes of Proverbs. Just try on these verses for size!

> *A gentle answer turns away wrath, but a harsh word stirs up anger. The tongue of the wise adorns knowledge, but the mouth of the fool gushes folly. The eyes of the Lord are everywhere, keeping watch on the wicked and the good. The soothing tongue is a tree of life, but a perverse tongue crushes the spirit.*
>
> **(Prov. 15:1–4)**

*Even fools are thought wise if they keep silent, and
discerning if they hold their tongues.*

(Prov. 17:28)

*Those who guard their mouths and their tongues
keep themselves from calamity.*

(Prov. 21:23)

I discovered the hard way how easy it is for characters like me to
hurt people with an unkind word and in my case, the one I have
hurt the most is my own wife in our 55 years of marriage together.
Before I was even married, due to God's work of grace in my life, I
was getting a very high level of victory with what was coming out
of my mouth, and the 'revolution of love' that I wrote about was a
growing reality in me. Through reading books like *The Calvary
Road* (CLC, 1980) by Roy Hession, *Humility* (CreateSpace, 2012)
by Andrew Murray and many more, I learned how to humble
myself, repent and apologise.

I realised that it was often pride that originally kept me from
doing that and at a young age I declared WAR on all forms of
pride. Verses like Galatians 2:20 became part of my spiritual
DNA and the lack of emphasis on the crucified life today in
some churches, and even among some leaders, is one of the
present-day weaknesses that concern me the most.

*I have been crucified with Christ and I no longer
live, but Christ lives in me. The life I now live in the
body, I live by faith in the Son of God, who loved me
and gave himself for me.*

(Gal. 2:20)

Again, Billy Graham was a huge help to me with the powerful messages of *'The Seven Deadly Sins'* and other radio sermons that I also got in printed form, read and distributed. *'The Seven Deadly Sins'* hit me so hard that I can tell you when and where I was when I read it: 8 Tasso Road, Fulham, London. We first lived there in a one-bedroom flat that Hoise Birks talks about in his autobiography *A New Man* (HB Publishing, 2012). It was February 1962 and we had just arrived in the UK and the name Operation Mobilisation was being used for the first time.

3. Laziness

I remember at an OM Conference in India back around 1967, I asked people to share their biggest struggle in their work and, to my surprise, they said laziness. I think this was such a big problem because of the extreme heat, and I experienced some of it myself. The early reading of Proverbs again had laid the foundation, and before I was 20 I had declared total war against lack of discipline and laziness in its many forms. Here are some great verses of encouragement:

> *Diligent hands will rule, but laziness ends in forced labour ... The lazy do not roast any game, but the diligent feed on the riches of the hunt.*
>
> **(Prov. 12:24,27)**

> *One who is slack in his work is brother to one who destroys.*
>
> **(Prov. 18:9)**

Laziness brings on deep sleep, and the shiftless go hungry ... A sluggard buries his hand in the dish; he will not even bring it back to his mouth!

(Prov. 19:15,24)

The sluggard says, 'There's a lion outside! I'll be killed in the public square!' ... Do you see someone skilled in their work? They will serve before kings; they will not serve before officials of low rank.

(Prov. 22:13,29)

I was fortunate in my childhood to have a very hard-working father and he taught me well in the biblical ethic of not being lazy. I had to learn again the hard way how to be patient with those that did not have that ethic and that just working hard for even one day would be quite a task for them. This strong emphasis on work and discipline could lead people into pretension and a sort of double life. People would behave one way when no one was watching, but quite differently when someone, especially on the team, was watching. Later they would feel condemned and that could lead to all kinds of spiritual and emotional confusion. This is why again and again our whole movement, and my own life, was rescued by 'radical GRACE'. Be sure to read Randy Alcorn's book *The Grace and Truth Paradox* (Multnomah, 2003) for help with this.

4. Anger

I started to get into fights at a young age, once even with a girl who sort of beat me up. I remember forming a little gang on my street in Wyckoff, New Jersey when I must have been around twelve. We fought with acorns that fell off the trees. Albert led the other gang and we were enemies. I wrote the most popular swear words of our day on the side of his big white house in black paint. Shirley, the girl across the street, must have seen me and told my dad. He really did not appreciate this early outbreak of art and I had to go and paint over it. It seems funny, but anger is not funny and it could have destroyed my life.

I remember visiting a man in prison who had killed a man. He went to his girlfriend's house by surprise and found another man with her. In a burst of anger he killed him on the spot. When I met him he had found forgiveness in Jesus and was pressing on in prison by sharing his faith.

Though I had a high level of victory in this important area, I also had my failures which to this day I remember well. Even as a child, down in my heart I never wanted to hurt anybody or anything. I felt bad when I killed a squirrel by mistake with my BB gun (or maybe it was with my bow and arrow? I cannot remember). I felt bad and gave the little animal a proper burial. Impatience, combined with anger, often in reacting to something, has been one of my weaknesses, but I have never given up the fight and learned the reality of 1 John 1:8–10:

> *If we claim to be without sin, we deceive ourselves and the truth is not in us. If we confess our sins, he is faithful and just and will forgive us our sins and purify us from all unrighteousness. If we claim we have not sinned, we make him out to be a liar and his word is not in us.*

The next verse in chapter 2:1–2 is also helpful:

> *My dear children, I write this to you so that you will not sin. But if anybody does sin, we have an advocate with the Father—Jesus Christ, the Righteous One. He is the atoning sacrifice for our sins, and not only for ours but also for the sins of the whole world.*

I feel so strongly about anger that I urge people to seriously consider whether to marry someone who does not have victory over anger, or if the person has had major anger problems in the past and there is a high chance that after marriage it will flare up again and there could be physical violence. Domestic violence, even among those who claim to follow the Lord, is one of the sins that the church has often been very gifted at covering up, especially if it's a deacon, elder or even the pastor or worship leader. If you are failing a lot in this area you need to get help. Just reading Proverbs will not be enough. You need help, which will always include repentance and walking in the light.

> *This is the message we have heard from him and declare to you: God is light; in him there is no darkness at all. If we claim to have fellowship with him and yet walk in the darkness, we lie and do not live out the truth. But if we walk in the light, as he is in the light, we have fellowship with one another, and the blood of Jesus, his Son, purifies us from all sin.*
>
> **(1 John 1:5–7)**

— — — — —

There is so much more on all kinds of vital subjects in this book and one of the main reasons for this chapter is to get you into reading the Bible regularly and dealing by faith with every issue that the Lord speaks to you about. I hope I get to hear from some of you who do just that (my email address is given at the end of the Introduction to this book). I hope you will also read 2 Timothy 2:2 and share what you have learned with others who can then, in turn, pass it on to even more people.

> *And the things you have heard me say in the*
> *presence of many witnesses entrust to reliable*
> *people who will also be qualified to teach others.*
>
> **(2 Tim. 2:2)**

I recently filmed a 'Book by Book' DVD on the book of Proverbs with Richard Bewes, Paul Blackham and the Biblical Frameworks team. I hope many of you will be able to watch it. Also a DVD of my life story, entitled *George – for real* (CWR, 2015), has been released by CWR and fits in very well with what I have tried to share in this book. For more information, or to order this DVD, please visit: **www.cwr.org.uk/store**. More of what I have written will become, I hope, even more alive and used by the Holy Spirit.

CHAPTER 3

Unity in the Midst of Diversity

I am in Germany as I type this chapter, at an unusual place. I'm at what is called the 'Mother House of the Deaconess Movement of Aidlingen', which is the village here. I have been coming here for about forty years. In a few weeks they will again put up a huge tent on their property and will have one of the largest youth events in the nation with more than 8,000 coming from all over the country to hear the Word of God and great Christian music. This year it is none other than our own, OM's Bill Drake. I remember speaking here some years ago and it always is amazing to see God working in the hearts of so many young people. These dear Sisters take vows of chastity and some think of them as Protestant Nuns though they are members of the Lutheran Church here in Germany. Wow, as a young Christian from the USA, I did not know that such people existed. I now consider it a great privilege to have some

35

of these Sisters in Jesus as close friends. This is one of my favourite places to have a change of pace and give myself to prayer, writing and some walking in the great forest where they are located. I also share the Word of God with them and have great fellowship around the wonderful meals they provide. Their deep love for Jesus and His Word and desire for world missions is very evident.

Can you imagine the diversity of movements, churches and people that I have come across in these sixty years in close to one hundred nations? Of course just spending time on our ship *Logos Hope* gives you about forty different nationalities together on one ship! No wonder the prayer nights are so especially interesting.

Wisley Gardens, outside London near Heathrow Airport, is another one of my favourite places. My close friend Danny Smith, who came to Jesus when I first met him in Calcutta almost fifty years ago, lives near there. He is always willing to pick me up at the train station and take me to this garden of thousands of different flowers. I have been there many times, often walking around listening to the Bible on audio or talking on the phone at the same time. The vast garden reminds me of the church across the world with now over 40,000 denominations/streams or movements, and it's going up fast!

One of my favourite sections at Wisley is the cactus section. I never knew there were so many kinds. Reminds me of many of the Lord's people I have met around the world.

I have heard leaders I respect speak about movements and denominations in a negative way and maybe I was of that mind a long time ago. But seeing the diversity of people the Lord used in the Bible and the variety of the stars and galaxies in almost every area of creation, I realise it's largely a wonderful and positive thing. I think the answer to why we are not all one church (although spiritually we are) is easy. That's not God's way of building His Kingdom (I know that means different things to different people) and we need to celebrate this great diversity. I know some of these movements may be heretical, so that counts them out as far as the Kingdom, but even there we may find some true believers in the midst of the mess. Most denominations have splits and the great global split is between those who believe the Bible is truly God's Word and those who don't. The word 'Fundamentalist' came into being to distinguish those who believe the Bible is the Word of God from those who did not, who often were called 'liberals' (nothing to do with politics). In more recent decades the word 'Evangelical' came to stand for those who hold to the biblical faith but who generally do not want the label 'Fundamentalist' which has been connected with hyper-legalism, judgmentalism and even compared to Muslim fundamentalists. That's why thousands of churches and hundreds of movements associate themselves with the WEA (World Evangelical Alliance) or the national counterpart in their own nation. I am part of the WEA and was active in my younger days. In our great global events we learned to respect even more the wonderful different ways God was working in so many denominations and movements.

I see them all as family and believe God does much of His work through family. I used to be hard on people who were not like me, interdenominational, but not anymore. If they know Jesus and are loyal to Him, their local church and maybe their denomination, I just say praise the Lord. That probably is where they found Christ and were brought up in the faith.

This is important to them and it's only normal that most of their spiritual life and activity will be among their own family.

We must face the fact that so much of church growth and also social concern and action take place on this basis. Yes, God uses interdenominational movements as well and we should be set free from the either-or mentality and realise that God works in different people in different ways.

Of course, the more we can have times of praise and worship and evangelism together, the better. For sure, without sincere love for one another we only hinder ourselves and our own church or movement.

God works through culture, language, people, situations and all kinds of circumstances. Most churches or movements over these last two thousand years were started by a visionary leader or leaders and there are thousands of examples. Up until Luther there were only a few major divisions but at the same time the Catholic Church learned how to channel diversity into different Orders and so we saw a huge range of Orders, like the Jesuits, Franciscans, Sisters of Mary. This is not the place for me to write about the great errors that had crept into that church in those days and until today. It was truly a 'messy' time, but would any of us dare to say God was not doing anything in the midst of it?

Catholics today are especially critical of all our different churches and denominations, but I recommend they go to Wisley Gardens. God works in our fallenness and humanity and so everything we humans touch, yes – even the Church, will have its weaknesses, faults and sometimes, sad to say, extreme and false doctrines. The mystery of mysteries is HOW our great God, because of what Jesus Christ did on the Cross, keeps working and doing wonderful things in the midst of it all. We must celebrate more of what our great God is doing across the world in, I believe, a million different local churches. Wow, to Him be the praise and glory!

This does not mean we lay aside our battle for greater holiness, reality, victory and all that I talk about in this book and in my other books. It does not mean that we forget that Satan is a roaring lion who seeks those he can devour and sometimes comes as an angel of light. The reality of the spiritual warfare outlined in Ephesians 6 is very real.

We are well aware that some churches and whole denominations are dead, or mainly dead. Others have crossed the line into extremism or even heresy. We must *all* fight the good fight. We must not make excuses for sin and folly, but always repent and try to put things right. Again, it is a balance of truth that is needed every step of the way.

In my previous book, *Drops from a Leaking Tap*, I especially deal with the tension that comes between the Church and the so-called para-church. I hope you will read that chapter (Chapter 22).

CHAPTER 4

Paradox, Complexity, Mystery and Messiology

I am very aware as I write this book that many young believers will read it and might find it quite over the top and even confusing in places. I have to take that risk because sooner or later we will all meet people, churches and Christian groups that are themselves over the top, confusing and possibly much worse. As you read my thoughts on many areas of Christian ministry and activity, no matter how sad, wild or even wrong it appears, the bottom line of this book is the greatness and mercy of God, because of what Jesus Christ has done for us on the cross. If you are struggling to understand me, it might be helpful to read John Stott's *Basic Christianity* (IVP, 2012) or Billy Graham's *Peace with God* (Thomas Nelson, 2000). You can email me and I will send some of these classic books as a gift.

Maybe you're among those young Christians who are already confused or even discouraged by what you have seen or even experienced in the church, OM or some other Christian agency. If so, please read on. Please try to see what I am trying to say as I want to share from my heart and mind some of the areas that I have struggled with, which have led to endless battles with disappointment, discouragement and even doubt and unbelief.

I guess one of the reasons I am writing this is that for sixty years in Christ I have listened to Christians and yes, often Christian leaders, who are so critical of other Christians, churches or organisations. This includes people I respect and love and from whom I have learned. My problem was not only that lack of concern and love that I saw, but that so often they did not have the facts right or they took things out of context. I wish that fifty years ago we had more books like *Leading with Love* (Lewis and Roth, 2006) by Alex Strauch or *If You Bite and Devour One Another* (Lewis and Roth, 2011) by the same author, a dear former 'OMer' that I have come to appreciate so much. We did have some books like that and I am so glad that in OM they were required reading. These books help lay our foundation more than we can know. This includes the unique book *The Calvary Road* by Roy Hession (which I have previously mentioned) and *Love is the Answer* (Back to the Bible, 1960) by Theodore Epp. Soon after I read that book, I wrote *The Revolution of Love* followed by books on discipleship, extremism and balance.

Let's make it clear that, especially as a young leader, I was sometimes one of the most critical of other leaders, churches or organisations. I slowly learned to be more positive, but it was only when I developed a different view of the way God works and who He works with that I was able to see positive things being done through people, churches or organisations that I felt had errors or wrong practices. In his book *The Grace and Truth Paradox*, Randy Alcorn has done us a great favour and showed us that we can have both strong commitment to truth, which I have always had, but also a life of love and GRACE. With this we will be much slower to criticise, especially when we really don't have the complete picture of the whole story. Facts are often hard to find.

At the same time, Scripture commands us to defend the faith. We could all be helped by a fresh look at John's second and third epistles.

In this chapter I want to share some of the areas that have caused so much confusion and struggle.

1. Books, leaflets and what I called the 'printed page' in my very first book *Literature Evangelism* (Authentic Lifestyle, republished in 2003). I first started selling books door to door as a young Christian of about two years in Christ. In the summer of 1957, before going to Mexico, a magazine called *Floodtide* by CLC came into my hands and my involvement with the Pocket Testament League, even before I was converted, all led me down the road of ministry through the printed page, especially through the Gospels, New Testament and the complete Bible. I was blessed reading Christian books and leaflets and wanted with total sincerity to bless others. In selling books door to door, I discovered that children's books sold the most so I got into that as well. I soon discovered all kinds of books with all kinds of teaching, some of which seemed very extreme and even untruthful. Looking back at a lifetime

with books I can shout, **God uses books**, but what you might not want to hear is that God can use bad books, and so can the devil. I discovered that books that I would not sell and did not like were used by God to help people and even bring people to Christ as Saviour. How do you handle someone being helped and blessed through a book that you believe is really bad? How do you explain God using books in a mighty way when the author has now fallen into adultery or worse? Even more complex is that books written by great men and women of God that we love and respect often disagree, and sometimes on important issues. If we read widely and respect a wide range of people, how do we decide in our heart what to believe? It seems easier for young believers and my grandson seems better than me at deciding what he believes on quite complex issues and doctrines. I will not be around, but I wonder how will he be at my age? At times it seems to be such a mess to me and I guess that is why I teach 'Messiology', that God in His mercy and grace and mystery often does great things in the midst of the mess, things that seem so very important to us and probably to Him. But what Jesus did on the cross reveals different priorities in the Living God in the way that He responds to different people, churches and situations.

2. If we think the world of Christian literature is complex then try television and the internet, such as YouTube, Facebook and all that's coming down the road. Forgive the cliché, but 'it blows my mind'. Research, including my own, will show that TV preachers, which some of us can hardly stand to watch or listen to, have helped not thousands,

but tens of thousands come to Christ all over the world. Now certain people immediately say, 'Well most of them must be false conversions.' Then we get a strong lecture on what the gospel is followed by an extreme statement of repentance and the Lordship of Christ to try to get us to believe that most of all, this is not biblical conversion. I have many problems with this but the big one is that I have met these people all over the world over the past fifty years and they do seem to be authentic believers. Many of them have been used of God not only to lead others to Christ but start thousands of churches.

Remember, we are still in the midst of the greatest harvest of people for the Lord that the world has ever known. As someone who was converted through a preacher who some have criticised, Billy Graham, I have had to live all my Christian life with the criticism that people who just make decisions in those kinds of meetings are not really saved, it's all just in the head. It has always been a mystery to me why some people almost seem to enjoy reducing the number of people who really are saved.

We say that people are saved by GRACE as they put their faith in the Lord Jesus Christ, but seem to indicate in our behaviour that keeping all the rules and regulations is really where it's at in terms of us knowing if you're a true Christian. Please try to read *Extreme Righteousness* (Moody, 1997) by Tom Hovestol and you will discover as I did how we strong believers in truth so easily develop a Pharisee streak. Swindoll's *The Grace Awakening* (and in particular, the chapter called 'Graciously disagreeing and pressing on') was such a huge help to me.

I myself keep my distance from certain people, including some famous ones, and distribute books against extremism like the extreme prosperity teaching. I still write and speak against false doctrine and extremism, but I would never tell God, the Living God, that He has to keep His distance from this or that person. I am a weak, very limited human being. He is the Almighty God of heaven and He seems to do mighty things in the midst of paradox, complexity and mystery. I call it 'Messiology' but you can describe it any way you want.

3. The third area I want to write about is music and the amazing way God has used and is using all kinds of music, songs and choruses to help people worship or come to Jesus. This has been another, over fifty-five years, saga of complexity. It's almost a miracle that from the beginning I was in favour of what has become labelled as 'contemporary music'. The New Testament does not say that much about music and the Old Testament seems to have quite a wide range of both music and dance. I still can't believe how much controversy came from this and how literally tens of thousands of churches around the world have had splits connected with this. On the one side some said, even writing in booklets, that drums are from Satan (I've got a copy). I listened to cassette tapes (back in the old days … oh dear, I still do now as my old car only has a tape deck) and read booklets and even whole books by some people that I respected, condemning much of the music that I personally saw God using in such a mighty way. This could have really discouraged me totally if I had not developed

a different view of God, His love and the way He works. He must have a great sense of humour as He watches the way His children behave.

If you think this music topic is a small thing or has gone away then I would say you do not know what is going on in the wider Church. Some have even lost their faith and walked away from the Christian Church and sometimes their own faith because of what they have seen in terms of extreme statements and harshness over the music issue. In the end it seems that the new and contemporary music has won the day … but it is not all over yet. Loudness presents a new set of problems and I do admit I carry earplugs almost everywhere. Quite a few key musicians falling into immorality or divorce has made an even messier scene, as well as musicians speaking strongly against other musicians which does not help. Some people seem to write off the whole Christian music industry with all kinds of stories about greed, pride and immorality. For me, this was a terrible mistake as in the midst of the mess, God was doing such a great work and so many were coming to know the Lord.

Those of us who read widely, especially Christian periodicals, will become over exposed to negative reports and Christian horror stories. Beware of proving a point by just telling negative stories as it is never the whole picture and never gives the full picture of what God can do in the midst of the mess and all our humanness. We all need to memorise Romans 8:28: 'And we know that in all things God works for the good of those who love him, who have been called according to his purpose.'

Where is God in all of this? I say right in the midst –

loving, forgiving, saving and using all kinds of what the Bible calls 'clay pots' to accomplish His purposes. Relax, now you don't have to leave your church with its traditional hymns, just stop condemning those who take a different road. I say to my peers in the sixties and seventies club, 'What is more important, that we enjoy the music or that more of the next generation come to know and worship Jesus?' Do we even have any idea of what God has done through churches like Hillsong and their music? Multiply this by 1,000 and you might get some idea of what our God is doing around the world through all kinds of music and people. Get yourself some earplugs and press on!

4. Lastly, I want to write about God's people in politics, right wing, left wing, no wings. In the USA right now this is an area of great controversy and division among God's people and it's getting worse by the day. One of my strongest beliefs is that God can work through a divided Church (speaking of the whole body of Christ) as that's all He ever had to work with. Why not try one of the Epistles in the New Testament for size? That, however, is never an excuse for a lack of love or any other sin. Much of the problem is linked with the fact that some people believe in the 'Christian nation theory' and others don't. I don't believe in the 'Christian nation theory', but love those who do. All nations in all times have operated in the midst of overwhelming evil. Those who believe that is all going to change in the future are deceived, but I love them as well.

    I majored in history before transferring to the Moody Bible Institute in Chicago and have studied history ever since. We can learn so much from history. Reading different viewpoints is hard and finding out what actually happened is even harder, so all history students should at least be humble and maybe a little less dogmatic. Should Christians engage in hate language and circulate hate emails? I don't think so, but if they do, somehow our mighty God still loves them and may use them more than I would ever want. So please don't get discouraged by the mess in this area or in the government, but try to focus on God and what He is doing in the midst of it. We have many thousands of years of history to show what God can do in the midst of a mess. Maybe we need to go and see the recent blockbuster film *Noah* (2014) and remind ourselves.

This does not mean we do not believe in being the salt and light, and certainly doesn't mean Christians should not get into politics or that there is no room for patriots. God works within our culture and these things are an important part of our culture. The more true Christian values we can see in society, including our own community, the better, but we cannot force them and legislate for them. We must not mix government with the church. Too many are fighting the dark these days instead of spreading the light. It's a losing battle and not worth all the effort. Let's get our priorities right. More than that, let's respect that God will lead different people and different churches in different ways. Why not go the extra mile in respecting God's guidance in other people? On many related issues we are never going to all agree, but I hope we can agree that our God can do great things in all kinds of situations, including those we would run away from.

CHAPTER 5

The Church, Missions and Hollywood

In the previous chapters I touched on just a few areas where things seem quite complex and messy. I am sure you don't want to read too much more along those lines, but let me briefly list some important others in this chapter. I have been reading and talking to people about all of these many areas for half a century, so bear with me a little. I believe understanding them will help you to be more grace-awakened, big hearted and forgiving. I believe you will have greater wisdom and discernment to handle tough situations, especially if you are a leader.

Church governance

I could have never believed as a young Christian how many different ways there are to lead a church and how the Lord seems to bless so many different methods. Often those who have a particular method believe in it very strongly and if you are among those I am not asking you to change, but maybe you will be a bit less dogmatic in thinking that your way of doing things is the only way. If we said things like 'one of the ways' it would be so much more sensible than saying 'this is the only way'.

We now have team-led churches and this concept is sometimes called elder-led, which goes back to the Brethren Movement that was such a dynamic movement in its day, and in some cases still is. Dale Rhoton, who I met at Maryville College and went to Mexico on that very first trip with me, became part of the Brethren Movement and wrote a booklet explaining that this was the New Testament way. I was only beginning to understand this unique movement, having first worshipped among them in Mexico City. William MacDonald who, at that time, was President of Emmaus Bible College in Chicago, was also becoming a friend and supporter. His book *True Discipleship* (Gospel Folio, 2003) became a great influence in our movement. There were many factors leading me to be baptised by immersion by Dale at Bethany Chapel in Wheaton. However, at that stage in my life I was already very, very interdenominational as Moody Bible Institute had helped me down that road. Then I went on to marry a Baptist, wow!

Dale and a few others were commended by their Assembly to work with OM and we considered that a great answer to prayer. Little did we know then that some years later I would end up starting the work in the UK, where the Brethren Movement was born and is still going strong. Historically, a number of our leaders, including our first UK Director, Keith Beckwith and later Peter Maiden, who became my Associate Director and then successor, were linked with them. The Brethren Movement has had many splits, almost every individual assembly has had one, but God keeps working and it is still a relatively healthy global movement. My acceptance by many of them, even speaking at major leaders events has been a huge encouragement. Some now have pastors who try to lead while still being a team player. Others are horrified by the idea and this has caused more splits. Let's be honest, in God's mysterious way of working, splits and division are one of the ways the church grows. That is not to excuse any sin or misbehaviour. Again, the concept of God working in the midst of the mess stares us in the face.

There is not space to go into all the different ways that churches are led. To the surprise of many of us, our work in India, totally under the leadership of Indians, chose to go more down a road that seems to combine the Brethren, Baptists, Methodists and the Anglicans with also a charismatic streak. The Good Shepherd Churches are one of the greatest fruits of our entire history, but we had to let them find their own way and my change of view on how our God works has helped me understand it more than I can express. You can be sure I am a raving fan and strong supporter of what's going on, but that does not mean I agree with it all or even understand it all. Whenever there are large numbers coming to Christ at once, it is not just a mess but a hyper, mega-mess! That's why we should pray and support more than ever that great work and other similar works. Through this rapid growth we have learned that *mistakes cost*. We also learned more about how the devil and his helpers can use gossip to try to destroy a work. Can we not all just be positive about the many ways that God works in such a variety of churches with different styles of leadership?

Hollywood and Christian films

I loved good films (and some bad ones) as a young kid and so it was quite a shock as a young believer to be told that films and the cinema are all from the devil! At Moody I had to sign a paper that I would not go to films. I was so strong for Jesus and world missions that in a sense I did not want to take any chances and on many issues I went along with the order of the day. Only later did I realise a lot of it was legalism and I was soon in its clutches. One thing is for sure, we have hundreds of years proving that God can work in the midst of a legalistic environment, but I believe the Bible teaches there is a better way. This is very linked with culture and the amazing way that God seems to be able to break into almost any cultural situation. When a Texan gets saved, he stays a Texan. That may irritate our Christian folks from Boston, but it's no big deal with the Living God. A lot of misunderstanding between states, nations and cities could be resolved if we were more God-centred and understood His amazing ways better.

Our movement ran parallel with the Christian Film Movement under the leadership of people like Ken Anderson and many others. Even in 1963 we had projectors in many of our lorries as we criss-crossed Europe, reaching millions with the Word of God. We have used films (then videos, now DVDs) in a major way ever since. I soon discovered that almost all those films were criticised especially by people in the film world. Of course most were low budget and so there were great limitations. History and heaven will show how millions came to know Jesus through these films. Does this not show us how God's thinking is so different from ours? We long for great things and better films of course, but meanwhile God is using what we would call not that good or even reject. Are we not way more judgemental and narrow-minded than the living God? Who do you think should change?

Church buildings

The money that is poured into church buildings with people dying of hunger and living in poverty all around the world is something that many cannot understand. The class system that went with it in the nineteenth century is almost beyond comprehension to Christian social radicals of our day. Whole movements were born partly reacting to it, like the Salvation Army and the Methodists. These movements, and many others, spread their faith around the world and so even in modern-day India and Pakistan we have huge buildings often tied up in legal cases, generally run down and looking very ugly. Yes, be careful if you're going to say that God is not working among the people in some of these buildings today.

Some of the largest new church movements also still have, to me, an unhealthy infatuation with nice and special buildings. It's a problem for me, but I don't really think it's a big deal with God. I wonder if you comprehend what I am trying to say? Some people get really upset if some of the old buildings are sold and become a mosque, for example. I personally think God is far more concerned about the people, including the Muslims, than He is about the old building. Why we are not loving and reaching out to our Muslim neighbours with the gospel is more what God might be asking us. Some of the churches that have been closed have been spiritually dead for years, turning away decades ago from the truth of Scripture, so why are we so worried? Even in places like the UK we have thousands of new churches and all kinds of Christian groups and surely that is more about what is on the heart of God today. There is a place for church buildings and I am sure all kinds of other buildings, but God will lead different people in different ways and very few will be impacted by the culture of their day including the church culture. I often find it upsetting but fortunately I don't think it's such a big deal with God.

CHAPTER 6

Must We Be So Dogmatic?

How hard it is for us strong-minded, committed, Bible-believing Christians to ever change. But we need to be willing to change if we have been wrong. Yes, without making some changes we can often become spiritually stuck and ineffective, often out of contact with younger people. Without change it makes it hard to pass on the vision and ministry to the next generation.

If we have been taught in a particular denomination, theological college or Bible college that will greatly impact us. We graduates might feel we have all our doctrine in cement. We sometimes think we have the answer to everything, even the hardest questions of life and theology. This to me is a great mistake. We must keep learning and growing and that often means admitting we are wrong. On the very basics of the Christian faith we must remain unmoveable, but on many issues in which there are a variety of interpretations, I believe it is better to not be so dogmatic. If we are, as the Bible says, to 'value others above yourselves'

(Phil. 2:3), then I think we must become more open to listening to others and willing to change.

Throughout the years I have met so many people who do not seem that interested in the fact that I am a believer in Jesus and saved by His grace. They seem to be more interested in whether I am Reformed, or Charismatic, or Arminian, or Baptist and the list goes on. Others want to know what I believe about the end times or the Jews or what translation of the Bible I use. I am not saying all this is irrelevant, but does this really please the Lord? Does this kind of mentality bring glory to God, which should always be what we want the most? Is there any hope for old guys like me who, after almost 60 years studying the Bible, Bible doctrine and yes, theology, are still not sure exactly what the truth is on some controversial issues in which great leaders that I respect and whose books I have read greatly disagree with one another?

All my life, I have struggled with the fact that so many who study theology lose their way and no longer believe the Bible is the Word of God. Sometimes referred to as 'liberal theology', it became dominant in the 1920s and 1930s in so many seminaries and colleges. Can we even begin to understand the impact of liberal theology in places like Germany, Switzerland, the Netherlands and yes, places like Sri Lanka and India, and of course the USA? In the light of this, should not those of us who believe the Bible stand in unity and not let so many smaller issues divide us? Embracing Messiology will help us do that for sure.

If there is more humility and less hyper-dogmatism on minor and controversial issues, then there would be less people reacting to it and falling into the deep pond of unbelief. In the end, people who are too dogmatic sometimes lose their faith all together. History proves this and I could have been one of them. What am I asking for? A change of attitude? Yes. More humility? Yes, and a different view of what God wants from us and our minds. Surely more fruit of the Holy Spirit and less unkind dogmatic remarks. Will we ever face the clear message that without LOVE we are NOTHING? Can there be more listening and higher esteem of those who believe differently, especially if they are basically people who still believe the Bible is the Word of God?

Recently one of our old-fashioned, hyper-dogmatic authors and preachers condemned the entire Pentecostal and Charismatic Movements, which is one of the largest movements in the entire, 2,000 years of the history of the Church. Amazingly enough, another great teacher/pastor and theologian wrote a book countering the first book. I am into both of them. Wow, what a ride! I believe the second book is closer to the truth and God's heart. It's called *Holy Fire* (Charisma House, 2014) by R.T. Kendall.

I have always written against extremes and so have many Pentecostals like Lee Grady of *Charisma* magazine, and this part of the Body of Christ seems vulnerable to say the least. But in my view they are one of the most faithful movements (with an incredible variety of denominations and churches) to believe the Bible is God's Word and with it faithfully preaching the gospel. That is why tens of MILLIONS have come to Jesus through their efforts and in answer to prayer.

Yes, they often add other teaching and some I feel are wrong. But I feel that this is true of most churches and movements in history. Surely God in His mercy still saves people in the midst of it all and I think saving PEOPLE is what really is on the heart of God. In order to drive forward our other teachings, and Pentecostals are very good at it, we underestimate the importance of so GREAT a salvation. I do find it a struggle that when my Pentecostals and Charismatic friends are under attack, they often fall into the same pit of being too dogmatic about things that are not that clear in the Bible and on which great men and women of faith have not agreed for centuries.

One group often attacks another group by telling horror stories about famous people (especially TV celebrities) who have failed and sinned in major ways. For years I have felt you cannot really prove things by Christian horror stories, even though they must be in the equation. God commands us to think more about 'whatever is true, whatever is noble, whatever is right' etc (Phil. 4:8). A leading conservative mission society has had workers convicted and imprisoned for paedophilia, which breaks our hearts, but that does not prove anything about the mission and the rest of the people. Just this morning I was studying David, Saul and Solomon. If you read Gordon MacDonald's brilliant book *Rebuilding Your Broken World* you will see that most Old Testament saints had what he calls 'broken world experiences'. Yes there are many areas where we need to be strong and unmoveable (some like the word dogmatic) but let's always stay humble and teachable and ready to change and become MORE LIKE CHRIST.

Do we only care for people as it's part of our job or do we really care for people because of the revolutionary work of GRACE in our hearts? This leads me to another question … do we mainly care for people when they are part of our organisation so that after they leave us in a few years we hardly remember their name, or do we make a commitment to love and care for them no matter where they may go? My research shows that many people after leaving a ministry or organisation soon feel forgotten. Oh, how the devil knows how to use that. He tries to get them to believe the organisation only used him or her. Most people say they don't have time to keep in touch with so many, but when I study people's lives and see how they waste time, it blows my mind. It is hard for us to face in reality our own self-centredness and lack of real dynamic, forgiving and practical love. I write this also for myself as I am a pilgrim, failure and learner.

CHAPTER 7

Romance, Marriage, Money and Much Mercy

I think by the age of thirteen, romance became the biggest thing in my life, only competing with sports and making money. The first gal I dated became my steady girlfriend. I think after dancing lessons we went to see *Quo Vadis* (1951) and only eternity will tell what kind of influence that film had on my young life. Around that same time dear Mrs Clapp, who lived across from my High School, put my name on her 'Holy Ghost Hit List', not only praying that I would become a Christian but also a missionary. Wow, she did not even discuss this with me! I actually had other plans for my life. I was already in business and thought about going into that kind of career.

An amazing girl called Lynn was a good influence in my life. She went to a Baptist church and I had no idea what that was. I remember her showing me the baptistery which seemed like a strange thing to me. I got to know and appreciate her parents and they were all a good influence in my life. Lynn and I danced and sometimes kissed up a storm but not beyond that, for which I am thankful as I look back. After we broke up, there were many other different gals that blew my romantic circuits and I am sad to say that around that time, in a small way, I moved into the world of so-called soft porn and lust. It was at this time that the Gospel of John, sent by Mrs Clapp and her son Danny, broke into my life. Also in my semi-liberal Reformed Church I had a godly Sunday School teacher who almost became a Jehovah's Witness but through the radio ministry of Dr DeHaan became a believer and as a result had an influence on me. After my conversion he was to become a lifelong friend, Fred Gnade. I especially remember his young sister Shirley, my next door neighbour from childhood there on Van Houten Ave, Wyckoff, New Jersey. She was the first girl I ever kissed – I guess we were six.

Jesus Christ, Madison Square Garden, Billy Graham and 3 March 1955 made all the difference to me. That night I was born from above and everything began to change. You can read something of those early days in the official history of OM, *Spiritual Revolution* (Authentic Media, 2008) by Ian Randell. I was new to the family of God and was soon to discover how different they were and how many rules had been brought into the game. It seemed that I was no longer allowed to kiss or dance, but I did not find any verses on that so kept doing both.

I was now 17, had my own car (a Henry J – wow, that really does date me!), and a senior in High School, when I fell head over heels for a gal named Margo, who was much younger and went to an Episcopalian Church. God was pursuing me big time as I was in the Word and starting to evangelise the high school where I had been elected President of Student Council. I was kept out of the National Honour Society due to my foolishness and clowning around, but in that final year my life was so changed that I was eventually accepted into that Society which was a big thing in our culture in that day. At the time, I did a really stupid thing. Parked off the road, sort of in the woods, Margo and I started to 'neck' (not sure if Americans still use that term) and as I started to move a little further, the police banged on the window and you can be sure I don't remember what the officer said. In my panic, I backed the car into a ditch and could not get it out. That was the worst night of my teenage years as her dad had to come to rescue us and, due to his maybe having had a few drinks, accused me of things we did not do and soon the relationship was over. I always felt bad about this as I know I hurt this young girl and soon lost track of her.

One more similar incident in a church parking lot was to bring an end to wild romance in my life; I am sure it's because people were praying. I decided on a 'cold turkey fast', no dating and no kissing (just the pillow a little), this went on for almost two years. The next girl I dated was Drena, who became my wife.

I had chosen to go to Maryville College partly because they had dancing after lunch every day. I never danced there and never dated there. It was there that much of my early growth in my Christian life took place. I was on fire for Jesus some people would say. Every extra hour when not studying I was out evangelising or praying, reading the Word or going to a Christian meeting. In an amazing way a Baptist pastor in a country church let me preach. Then the door opened for ministry in the Blount County Jail which, when I was only 18, opened the door to share the Word at the Nashville State Penitentiary.

Great books came into my life like *The Passion for Souls* (Welch, 1986) by Oswald Smith and *Through Gates of Splendour* (Authentic Media, 2005) by Elisabeth Elliot and many more. I was greatly impacted doing a correspondence course on how to lead people to Christ. When that same Baptist pastor took me to my first mission conference down the road in Chattanooga at a Bible College named Tennessee Temple, I was to never be the same. Even before my conversion because of the Gospel of John, and the Pocket Testament League that published and distributed it, I wanted to see everyone, everywhere, have that great book. As a 'baby' Christian I got about 1,000 of my fellow High School students to promise to read it. As I found out about more nations and how so many were so unreached, the vision for reaching them, and especially Muslims, began to grow in my heart and mind. When I started to realise that finance was urgently needed I starting selling everything I could and gave the money to world missions. I got a job waiting on tables in the college restaurant in order to be able to give more.

It was during this period that we first went to Mexico in the summer of 1957. I was soon speaking poor Spanish and the impact of what I saw and other factors caused me to want to leave the Liberal Arts Maryville College and go to Moody Bible Institute in Chicago. I especially wanted to live and evangelise in the Big City. I had a taste of it near my home when I went distributing thousands of tracts in the underground subway system in New York City and then, just before we went to Mexico, I got involved in the famous Billy Graham Campaign. I even preached in the streets there.

Arriving at a place like the Moody Bible Institute was a big shock, especially seeing so many attractive girls. I must have been infatuated with several in the first week, but I kept to my promise and proceeded with my cold turkey romance fast. Looking back, I wonder whether, if I had tried to kiss one, they would have hit me with their big King James Bible! Of course Moody had a rule book and there seemed to be strict rules for everything.

My passion for evangelism led me to get a film from the Moody office up on the 7th or 8th floor; little did I know this would be the day that would change my life. Drena was sitting at the desk in charge of that office. When I saw her my romantic circuits blew and I broke my fast, moving in on the target. For me it was love at first sight, but as soon as I said something rather stupid, for her it was fright at first sight! Nothing happened but she did agree to meet. That's when I told her, 'Well nothing is probably going to happen between me and you, but if anything did, like say marriage, you need to understand that I am going to be a missionary and you probably will be eaten by cannibals in New Guinea'. How she eventually agreed to marry me is a long story, including a difficult summer together in Mexico City, then leaving her behind when I went back to Moody. This led to my best Mexican friend falling in love with her and phoning me up to ask if that was okay. Wow, this led me to some serious fasting and prayer. After a phone call with Drena, she was soon on a long bus journey back to Chicago.

In all of this I was deeply convicted of my lack of practical love and sensitivity. Drena was discovering herself and her deep emotional needs. Our engagement might have broken if it were not for a deep experience she had with Jesus in the quiet of her own room as she understood something of the all-sufficiency of Jesus. This also led to a healing experience of some physical symptoms that had bothered her for a long time.

We will never forget that big day, 31 January 1960, when we got married. We did not have anything fancy, keep in mind that Drena's stepfather Henry was not a Christian. The story of his conversion to Jesus many years later is something we will always thank God for. We had the marriage ceremony right after the Sunday morning service of Lake Drive Baptist Church. They did not have their own building, so this was in a school gymnasium. Walter Borchard was my best man. A bus came up from Chicago with our friends, mainly Moody students. Dale preached a powerful message at the reception mentioning that the best thing they could do for us was pray as we probably would sell all the gifts for world missions. How I wish we had not lost that old reel-to-reel tape with that message.

As we look back at fifty-five years of marriage, what can we share that might be of help to you who are reading this? Back around 1970, I was going to write a book about marriage and had decided on the title, *The Revolutionary Marriage*, and even had an outline. The truth is I needed to learn more about making our own marriage work rather than writing about it. Here are some of the lessons I have learned along the way:

1. Our marriage is based on the Bible. This has been the practical foundation of our marriage, always wanting Christ at the centre of everything. Living on the floor in the back of our Mexico City book store when we were first married, brought some challenges and I was to learn fast that marriage was really God's PhD programme in sanctification. We read

'Revival in the Home', one of the chapters in Roy Hession's *The Calvary Road* and learnt more about brokenness, humility and the Spirit-filled, crucified life. Over all these years, again and again I knew I had just the right person to be my life partner and by His grace we have been totally faithful to one another, where many now seem to laugh at that. From the Bible we saw no other alternative. Bring onto centre stage the lostness of people and their need to be reached, this impacts us on a daily basis.

2. The idea of the Revolution of Love – which we write and preach about and try to practise with 1 Corinthians 13 and other scriptures as the foundation, has been one of the most important aspects of our marriage. I especially tended towards extremism and insensitivity and God has had to break that down and deal with me. Impatience has been a problem all my life. My hatred of sin and any kind of pride helped me to humble myself and quickly repent. The miracle of grace that set me free from anger in the earliest days of my walk with God was a major factor in our walk together and in my leadership of the movement. There were still occasional failures that had to be quickly repented of, but to this day I feel sad about the times I hurt my wife and later my own children with a burst of anger or an unkind word. Arriving in England from Spain where Benjamin, our first son, was born was a big step for us. At that time, reading Billy Graham's important work *Freedom From The Seven Deadly Sins* (Zondervan, 1963) humbled me and how I thank the Lord for this book. As I have mentioned before, I also used to read his radio sermons all the time

as a young Christian. Other books by him like *Peace with God* and *The Secret of Happiness* (Thomas Nelson, 2002) were all keys in laying the foundation in my life.

3. Our desire to reach people with God's Word locally and around the world, combined with starting a whole new missionary movement, always brought financial pressure and challenges and led me into extremism that God seemed to use but also seemed to confuse some people and my own wife along the way. I emphasised Luke 14:33 'In the same way, those of you who do not give up everything you have cannot be my disciples.' That challenge had already led us to sell most of our possessions. Others followed us in this but it sometimes led to being judgemental of those who seemed to be wasting money. We needed the balance that Philippians 4:19 would supply. We were starting to learn more about the mystery of how things that seem so good can have a dark side. Grey started to come into our previously more black and white world and has been on the increase ever since. Can you guess why the last verses of Romans 11 have been so important to us?

Oh, the depth of the riches of the wisdom and knowledge of God! How unsearchable his judgments, and his paths beyond tracing out! 'Who has known the mind of the Lord? Or who has been his counsellor?' 'Who has ever given to God, that God should repay them?' For from him and through him and for him are all things. To him be the glory for ever! Amen.

4. The biggest mystery as we moved down the marriage road was seeing so much unanswered prayer even in areas that are hard to talk about. We started to battle with large attacks of discouragement often linked with disappointment. The years with three children living in India, the years in Kathmandu, Nepal and then in *Logos*, gave us endless opportunities to learn and grow together. I felt Drena's help and affirmation through it all and remember very few complaints even in the midst of the heat of the battle.

5. Depression somehow came into Drena's life in the mid-1970s which took us all by surprise. A woman confronted me during that time pointing out that I was probably part of the problem. God broke me and showed me changes that needed to take place in my own life and the way I behaved as a husband and father. After a year, Drena came out of this dark period and it never came back. We are sad at the simplistic answers some Christians and even books give to these complex illnesses and in my view, extreme teaching on healing (and I believe God heals) have hurt more people and the body of Christ as a whole more than we will ever know. One church in the USA that went to the ultimate, 'no doctors ever' extreme has their own cemetery and even twenty-five years ago there were over seventy buried there, mainly children.

6. Handling criticism is an important part of leadership and I sometimes found it difficult and felt personal hurt. I never heard much criticism of our marriage or my wife, but we

found it hard to handle what we did hear, often second-hand. A major part of leadership and your walk with God will be tested to the core when your marriage is criticised. In God's mercy, I am sure we never actually hear some of the worst gossip and criticism, especially if you're in the fast lane trying to evangelise the whole world. I was greatly blessed by always having loyal people like Dale Rhoton and Peter Maiden and others who I know often came to my defence. It is much harder for leaders who do not have such faithful friends and co-workers.

7.   As I look back, I realise I learned so much from my critics and from close friends who would walk in the light with me about something they saw in my life and ministry that needed change. God showed us from His Word and Christian books that it is not possible to do anything without criticism. We always tried to love our critics and ask for God's blessing on them. We were never surprised at the power of gossip. The truth is that we were/are happy and fulfilled most of the time, even right into these unique senior years when many things change especially in the area of health. We are fortunate to have so many people praying for us and some of you who are reading this are in that category. We thank you with all our hearts and hope you will keep on praying.

8.   Balance became one of the most important words in our lives. Balance between work and family. Balance between taking in and giving out. Balance between giving and receiving. Balance in terms of going the extra mile to reach more people

and slowing down to have family fun and time. In my old Bible I had a couple of lists that were working for balance. One of my books had the original title of *The Revolution of Love and Balance*.

9. Children and grandchildren always help change your life. We are thankful to God for our three children and five grandchildren. At this time they do not all follow the Lord Jesus, but we love them and try to be the best parents and now grandparents that we can be. We have wonderful and amazing times together including trips and holidays. To be honest, we are very aware of failure and realise the subtleness of what I now call 'unrealistic destructive idealism'. When we set high goals as we have, we will fail. Some non-Christians would not even think of some of these things as failures. This is why books like Philip Yancey's *What's So Amazing About Grace?* (Zondervan, 2002) and Swindoll's *The Grace Awakening* have been so important to us. And what can we say of the breath of fresh air of *The Ragamuffin Gospel* (Multnomah, 2005) by Brennan Manning who recently went to be with the Lord? In those early days especially, legalism had entered our Movement and also our home and some damage was done. We have to now practise 1 Peter 5:7 and 'cast all your anxiety on him because he cares for you' and accept His forgiveness. Without RADICAL forgiveness, radical discipleship will never work.

CHAPTER 8

Mistakes Cost

I owe so much to my parents who may not have known Jesus personally during my childhood, but who had many Christian values and taught us right from wrong. They helped me learn how to work hard, even from an early age, which laid a vital foundation in my life before I ever came to Jesus. Working hard at school, in sports and in the Boy Scout Movement also helped me more than I probably realise. The Scouts sent me on an Advanced Leadership Training course when I was very young. Tell me, do you think the Living God was preparing me for something I could have never imagined at that young age?

I learned quickly that mistakes can cost and bring difficulty in more ways than one. I made a mistake as a little boy by balancing a penny on my nose which I then proceeded to swallow. My mother insisted that I come home from school every time I had to go to the toilet. The Washington Primary School was near our home at 243 Van Houten Ave, Wyckoff, New Jersey and so we got the penny back! I made another mistake on a frozen lake during ice skating season and fell through the ice. Somebody grabbed me and pulled me out. We have read of others who made that mistake and lost their lives.

All my life, especially after becoming a follower of Jesus, I have been an avid reader. What I have read includes books, newspapers, magazines, articles and now endless email attachments, which is helping me write this book. Watching many films and DVDs, especially documentaries, has also been a huge help. No book has been more important than the Bible which I believe is God's Word. The Bible is filled with stories of great success and great failures and we need to learn from both.

It seems that, no matter what you read, you are always reading about mistakes people make. I think as believers in Jesus it is important that we don't think all mistakes are sin. They may have some roots in our fallen nature, but they are not always outright sin that we must immediately repent of. Satan likes to use our mistakes to get us discouraged or down on ourselves. When we allow ourselves to get down and discouraged we open ourselves up to sin or wrong attitudes and behaviour and then we get into much more trouble spiritually. So, the big lesson is that when we make a mistake, we must bounce back, look for Plan B and press on. We could all be helped by the book *Second Choice* (Paternoster, 2000) by Viv Thomas.

History shows the domino effect of mistakes, with one mistake leading to another. In 1988, we lost our first ship, *Logos* (which was once was home for our whole family, thank the Lord for its seventeen years of vital ministry), on some submerged rocks in the Beagle Channel in the very south of

Chile and Argentina. Research showed a series of mistakes by different people led to that fateful day. However, God was merciful and there was no loss of life and He used the publicity from the mistake, which was national news – especially in the UK, to help get the funds for a much better ship, *Logos II* (which later led to *Logos HOPE*). I don't want to take time here to also write about the terrible car accidents over these over fifty-seven years, always caused by yes, you guessed it, MISTAKES.

History also shows that everyone makes mistakes and for sure, the LESS MISTAKES, THE BETTER. We must not allow what we believe about the sovereignty of God, or what I call Messiology to keep us from a strong common sense commitment to do things right and make as few mistakes as possible. I wish that somehow at Bible College I had been warned just how hard life is and how many problems and difficulties we would all face. We need to reread and study James 1 and 1 Peter 1 and many other passages. I never realised how for so many people just to have the money to buy food is a huge thing and takes a lot of discipline and hard work.

> *Consider it pure joy, my brothers and sisters, whenever you face trials of many kinds, because you know that the testing of your faith produces perseverance. Let perseverance finish its work so that you may be mature and complete, not lacking anything. If any of you lacks wisdom, you should ask God, who gives generously to all without finding fault, and it will be given to you.*
>
> **(James 1:2–5)**

Throughout our ministry, we seemed, including in OM, to over emphasise prayer, faith and spiritual life giving the false impression that if we have it all together in those areas everything will work out okay. Now, looking back at sixty years in Christ, for so many people that I have followed over the years it has NOT TURNED OUT OKAY! There are quite a few who, after the faith, prayer and evangelistic life of OM, returned home and could not get a job or hold one down. Some of the marriages of people who met on OM have broken, often because they had not thought about some of the problems that would face them in the future. Put this together with other mistakes we easily make and you have a formula for trouble, often big trouble. Many have not been successful in their ministry or jobs or even in their marriages. I meet such people all the time and try to share radical grace. I say, 'If you have failed a lot and missed Plan A, then praise the Lord that Plan B can be just as good'. Some have made many mistakes and had many failures and feel they are probably on 'Plan H or M'. I say, 'Praise the Lord for a big alphabet'. People usually laugh at this point but in the end it's not funny. Those mistakes could have been avoided. We could have saved ourselves and others a lot of trouble. We must beware of any kind of fatalism in any of its forms. We must take seriously all the Bible teaching in all kinds of spiritual and practical areas, otherwise why have the book of Proverbs?

Sin is in so many ways more serious, but so often our mistakes are a combination of sin and old-fashioned stupidity. Or, to be more gentle, a lack of wisdom and discernment. One of the reasons I have read so widely is to learn from the mistakes and failures of others and in my lifetime have read about thousands of them.

Here is what I have learnt about how we can avoid mistakes:

1. Saturate ourselves with God's Word, giving ourselves to prayer and all aspects of our spiritual walk with God. I have shared that in all my other books. I would be happy to send them as a gift, please email me if you are interested.

2. Learn discipline in all the basic areas of life – try to beware of legalism every step of the way.

3. Learn how to read and study hard. Have a system to remember important information.

4. Learn how to write things down. If you travel, have a list of things you must not forget. New types of phones and other gadgets can help, but it still demands discipline.

5. Plan ahead and count the cost as we are urged to do in the last verses of Luke 14. I could write a whole chapter on this important concept and some of the biggest mistakes I have seen are in this area. All kinds of people have come to me and shared their great vision and dreams but most of them never materialise or last long. Often they did not count the cost or they were not ready to pay the price.

6. When you have time, try to think of the pros and cons for a particular step or action you are about to take.

7. Try to seek advice. This has its downside like so many things in life as you can get wrong advice, so do always weigh up personal prophecy carefully.

8. As much as possible, plan ahead. Double check all times, dates and try to calculate what you will do if things go wrong. Have a Plan B in the back of your head. If I travel by train, I always try to take an earlier train than the one that would just make it on time.

9. Many of our mistakes are made when we are on the move. In one way we have to learn to be professional travellers learning from our mistakes and the mistakes of others. Once in Frankfurt Train Station when I was on my own I took my eyes off my briefcase (for less than a minute!), it was gone and I never saw it again. Fortunately, the thief did not get my laptop or too many valuables. As much as possible keep valuable things on you. What about a money belt or some kind of waist bag? Sad to say in all of this, life is more difficult for women than men and I leave women to write about that. Be sure you have photocopies of credit cards, passports etc.

10. Since, sooner or later, we all leave valuable things behind, we should develop a strategy not to do that. For example, after you leave a room go back again and double check that you have not left anything behind. Especially check all electric sockets to see if you have left a phone or charger plugged in. In all of this, the more we can be in twos, rather than on our own, the better. Learn how to check on one another and learn from each other. Let pride die and walk in humility ready to quickly confess weakness.

11. Have a good system with a backup for all addresses, phone numbers, etc. Have a system for filing things. My folders on my laptop are now a key part of my life. What a great tool to use in God's work. I have a little black back-up book for phone numbers and you cannot imagine how much this is used. If we really love people and want to encourage them, we will go the extra mile to keep their basic information. ORGANISE, ORGANISE, ORGANISE! Gordon MacDonald's book *Ordering Your Private World* (Thomas Nelson, 2012) has helped a lot of people. If you read widely you will find all kinds of practical advice on almost every aspect of life and it is in itself a great mistake not to learn from it.

12. Learn what I call the 'Holy Ghost Caution'. There was a wonderful missionary who was out walking in the hills of England, but he did not have on the right kind of shoes. He walked too close to the edge of a cliff, slipped and fell to his death. I will never forget getting the phone call the next day about this dear friend's death. Another missionary friend's wife slipped on a hill near a cliff and fell to her death. If I shared another few hundred similar stories that I know about, you would understand better why I am taking time to write this book and especially this chapter. I have no doubt that if people take heed of what I write here that I will save lives and I really love doing that.

You can of course add to this list or make your own, but I must not take up more space here. You may think this 'how to' guide is not important in comparison to all the spiritual messages about the Christ-life and discipleship, but that kind of separation of the so-called sacred from the practical is a great mistake in our thinking. We must bring it all together under the power and guidance of the Holy Spirit. We are created in the image of God. We have a free will and on a human level we will decide our destiny. You decide each hour of each day what you will do, where you will go and how you will behave. We must grow and mature in every area of life. Even at my age there are lessons to learn.

Each great biblical reality and teaching must be relearned at different phases of our life. We must not just live well, but learn and be ready to die well. As we get older we must watch out for the 'SSS'. Someone asked me the other day what this means, 'Oh,' I said, 'it's *Senior Stupidity Syndrome.*' The problem is that now in our culture it has spread to every age group.

I close this chapter with these great words from James 1:22: 'Do not merely listen to the word, and so deceive yourselves. Do what it says'. I recommend a good study of the book of James.

CHAPTER 9

The Leaders God Uses

I am typing this chapter in a special place on the west coast of Wales, called the Hookses, where one of the great Christian leaders of the twentieth century did a lot of his writing, Dr John Stott, who became a close friend, and whose books to this day have global influence. I hope you will read many of them. It's sad that especially in the USA, with certain people, if you mention John's name they bring up how he denied the existence of hell and especially eternal punishment, which is not true at all. He believed people outside of Christ were lost. I spoke to him personally about it. In one of his books, written especially to answer the tough questions that some liberal theologians were asking, he touched on the possibility of some kind of annihilation and we also spoke personally about this too. Many great men and women of God have struggled with exactly what hell is like. I remember Billy Graham saying it was mainly separation from God.

I have tried every day to live my entire life since my conversion, in the light of this truth which I still don't fully understand. I have been helped by meditating on the justice of God. Universalism is more popular than ever, but John Stott did not go down that road and I am sure it's one of the reasons he was so committed to global missions. I heard him say in a great mission message that one of the great battles of the Church in our day was the exclusiveness of the gospel. Jesus says, 'I am the way and the truth and the life. No one comes to the Father except through me' (John 14:6).

That leads me to the main thrust of this chapter. It's a plea to understand better the wide range of people that God uses in leadership, both men and women. Can you imagine the number of leaders I have met and whose churches I have spoken in? Add to this all the different kinds of leaders I have known in mission agencies and other organisations. Yes, it's in the thousands, and yes I have listened to thousands of messages, many of them on tape or some other audio form. Plus, I have read about all the main leaders mentioned in the Bible.

We have a huge range of books on leadership and endless autobiographies and biographies of men and women of God right back to the beginning of time. I have read and reviewed many, and taken a look at even more. They are now coming at us faster than ever and one of the most important parts of my own ministry is speaking to leaders and also distributing outstanding leadership materials. The two top books at present are *Spiritual Leadership* (Moody, 2007) by J. Oswald Sanders which is in many languages and *Leading with Love* by Alex Strauch. I have expressed some of my own views strongly in my booklet 'Grace Awakened Leadership' which in fact is two key chapters taken from my book *Out of the Comfort Zone*.

Again, if you don't embrace what I call Messiology you will

probably not agree with what I try to share here. I am strongly convinced that God works mightily through a wide range of different leaders and different leadership styles.

Some books and teachers have very high ideals for leadership and some are so dogmatic that other styles, different from the one set forth in their books, are condemned or looked down upon. I try to warn people about this destructive idealism that leaves out the radical grace factor and eventually leaves people discouraged, confused or even wiped out completely.

History proves otherwise. All kinds of leaders and leadership teams have been mightily used to bless, disciple and teach His people and bring tens of millions to the Lord Jesus around the globe. We are key distributors of Chua Wee Hian's book *Learning to Lead* (Authentic India, 2010) but for decades also watched how he led a key church that he founded in London after being the international leader of the whole of the IFES Movement. Put that with David Lundy's book *Servant Leadership for Slow Learners* (Paternoster, 2002) and you have a unique combination. I have noticed that many leaders who have actually accomplished the most have not followed this style. They often have been more autocratic and usually get accused, at least some, of being dictatorial or even abusive. I've read a book about abusive leadership in which as far as I could see, almost every dynamic leader who tries to persuade people with some passion and emotion to serve and love Jesus with all their heart, mind, soul and strength, will be considered abusive. Some people when they come under that kind of person do not want to accept the strong message and then in some cases will try to find some weakness in the person giving the message. If we are honest there are many biblical verses, when we read them out loud, that seem to be abusive. Try 'I know your deeds, that you are neither cold nor hot. I wish you were either one or the other! So, because you are lukewarm – neither hot nor cold – I am about to spit you out of my mouth' (Rev. 3:15–16). And then Luke 14:33, 'In the same way, those of you who do not give up everything you have cannot be my disciples.'

We really need a lot of wisdom on how we use that strong word 'abusive'. I remember a woman on one of my teams years ago that I thought was rushing into marriage and when I tried to just slow her down a little she turned on me and accused me of being a control freak . After that hurtful conversation, I stood with her and even attended the wedding and reception only to see within a couple of years the marriage come to an end.

One thing for sure that I must say is, after sixty years in some kind of leadership, that at its best leadership is very difficult. All of us as leaders are imperfect and have our weaknesses that sometimes lead to clear-cut sin. All the people we try to lead and help also have weaknesses leading sometimes to sin and so what will the result be? Often one big mess! Hurt people, broken hearts and disappointments. So many who come under our leadership today have already been hurt so much, sometimes even sexually abused, that it's extremely hard to lead and help them. Most leaders are busy and overcommitted and often it's because they are trying to love and serve Jesus and His people. Add to that, effort to evangelise and have many non-Christian friends, and you are looking at the impossible. Things will go wrong. People will be hurt. That is why for me, without the burning reality of 1 Corinthians 13 flowing in our hearts and the humility and brokenness that goes with it, it often becomes impossible to move forward. I have seen and read of hundreds of leaders who have fallen out with each other. I have seen a deputy leader try a pull a coup or overthrow the so-called number one. When the wife, or husband, gets involved, it becomes even more bizarre.

It takes a high level of spiritual reality from strong-minded leaders to work together. Some leadership books leave out the message of the Cross and the crucified life:

> *'I have been crucified with Christ and I no longer live, but Christ lives in me. The life I now live in the body, I live by faith in the Son of God, who loved me and gave himself for me.'*

(Galatians 2:20)

I heard someone say that the fastest reason for Church growth was all the Church splits. The idea that God cannot work when there is sin in the camp sounds good and some may think there is an Old Testament story to back it. Only one major problem! It's just not true. 2,000 years of church history show that God is doing great things and saving multitudes of people in the midst of sinful, messy situations.

Let's beware of being too narrow minded in regards to our feelings about how God works through people. We can have our convictions on how we should lead, but be slow to criticise people who have a different style. Different churches have all kinds of leadership forms. Yes, I personally believe some are better than others, but it is much harder to measure that than I once realised. There is hardly a single church or Christian mission or organisation that has not had its messes and its problems and yes, its sinful behaviour. In some cases I make a firm decision to pull back and stay away. **But, I cannot tell the Living God to stay away**. He will continue to amaze us with the way He uses all kinds of leaders in all kinds of situations, including the very messy ones. Yes, it's Messiology on a grand scale.

Some who read this will not be convinced, but if I could sit with you and share the more than a thousand incidents I have seen and read about that have moved me down this road, then I think you might become even more convinced than I am. If you are very young you will also find this hard and even confusing. However, please don't wait until you get old to learn these valuable lessons. Get into good books on leadership now, starting with the Bible itself.

CHAPTER 10

Worship, Walking and Wonder

I have just been walking and worshipping here by the Hookses where John Stott must have walked, prayed and watched birds many times. I took a look in his office and cottage where he must have spent some amazing times. Many of his books were on the shelves including his two-volume biography. I found a new book that I had not seen before, edited by Chris Wright who is now the leader of the Langham Partnership, who own this place. It's called *John Stott: A Portrait by His Friends* (IVP, 2011). I wish I could just sit down and read it all.

I have walked the Pembrokeshire Coast many times especially with my very special Welsh friend Wayne Thomas who was introduced to me by Doug Burton who founded The Haven not far from here in Pembroke. Wayne was far from God, often living a high life with lots of drink and all that goes with it. He was delivering cakes to The Haven and met a former stuntman from the States named Chuck

Cox, which led to his powerful conversion. Doug told him to go to one of my meetings in Carmarthen and after the meeting he drove me a long way back to a farm in the Quantocks outside Taunton. This is a place where Drena and I went most years for a change of pace and a break as it was managed by Dave and Mary Hawthorne who had become very close friends. It was the beginning of a lifelong friendship. We often walked these coastlines together. Wayne ended up joining OM, working with me and met a wonderful OM worker in France, Hilary, who he later married and they became the leaders and caretakers of our OM Retreat/Conference Centre in West Watch, West Sussex. They now, alongside their two grown-up daughters, minister at our USA base in Tyrone, Georgia.

Walking and, for quite a few years, jogging has been an important part of my life. I often combine them with praise, prayer and worship. I find it easier to worship out in the midst of God's creation than in some kind of building filled with people, but of course I believe in both. Being alone with God has been a major part of my handling stress and all the challenges of leadership. I am especially fascinated by water, canyons, gorges and rugged coast lines.

My favourite places, competing with the Swiss Alps (especially on trains dictating letters), are all the National and State Parks in Southern Utah and Northern Arizona, including Bryce, the Arches, Zion and the Grand Canyon. God in His mercy and love has let me visit these places many times with many different people including my children and grandchildren.

I am actually currently sitting on an inside window ledge looking out over the beautiful coastline with Milford Haven somewhere in the distance, where I remember the *Logos* visited many decades ago. It is my prayer that many of you will read *The Logos Story* (Paternoster, 1992) and *The Doulos Story* (BookRix, 2014) by Elaine Rhoton and now *Logos HOPE* (BookRix, 2014) by Rodney Hui and George Simpson. You will be amazed at how the Lord has used the ship ministry. Who knows, you might even end up serving on an OM ship one day.

My mind jumps back to John Stott and I ministering together on *Logos II* in London. He and I were very different and when he first heard me speak in Urbana in the late 1960s he was quite upset with the lack of Bible content in my message (it was mainly my testimony) and when he confronted me I started crying. Little did we know that it was the beginning of a lifelong friendship. The more we spoke or ministered together the more we realised how much we had in common and he became a great supporter of OM. What a joy recently to preach at All Souls Church where he was the leader and rector for so many years.

I write all of this to encourage people to find balance in their lives. I hope you have read about this in some of my other books, but I cannot overemphasise the importance of it, especially finding the right balance between the aspect of work and ministry which you find quite draining with ministry and activity that you find really refuels you.

Even in your Bible study it is vital to let one strong Scripture be brought to its true perspective by other pieces of Scripture. Taking verses out of context, especially from the Old Testament and hitting people on the head with them is not the way to go. I never cease to be amazed at the misuse of Scripture, especially the Old Testament. We of course take the verses we like and leave out the verses we don't like or don't understand. I find it heart-breaking to see so many friends and believers getting into different extremes and tangents. People get caught up with different extreme views often circulated by all kinds of extreme one-sided emails that seldom give the full picture and both sides of the story.

When I meet such people they often seem very negative and even bitter and angry. Talking to such people makes me think that selective reading (reading only one side of issues) seems worse than not reading at all. Everyone with any education and experience knows you cannot believe everything you read, even Christian books, magazines and papers exaggerate or get it wrong sometimes. Even some major papers are dominated by only one viewpoint. There are endless cults and extremist groups propagating their 'thing' all over the world. Apologies sometimes come, but so often in such small print that most people miss them. Some hot emails and blogs have been proven totally false. All kinds of conspiracy theories are flying around, some as old as the hills and some very new. Health, religion and politics are the big areas of endless generalisations, half-truths, over-reactions and pure nonsense. When people are locked into a particular political party (not necessarily wrong) they sometimes find it impossible to see some positives that the other parties may be saying or doing. I often find such a lack of common sense and balance in what people say and that includes a lot of the preaching that I have listened to.

People are often unable to understand how much their own temperament and hurts affect what they believe and speak about. Of course, black and white thinkers are especially vulnerable in this world of so much grey. As committed believers in Jesus and His Word we have basic issues where we feel it's clear black and white. There are areas where black and white thinking is needed, 'You shall not murder' (Exodus 20:13) for example, and yet even there, there are Christians who are not in agreement, especially about weapons and war. I have upset people who, after they set forth their great opinion about something I then point out the complexity. The fact that I have spent seventy years reading, studying and ministering in thousands of churches in almost one hundred nations does not seem to mean much. The thing that is really scary is that when some people keep going down an extreme road, they seem to become neurotic (if they aren't already) and how sad the whole thing becomes.

I fear within the Church, we are birthing a whole new brand of Pharisees, which also brings division, confusion and in the end discouragement and a loss of faith. This even happens within families. Can we not, with our strong convictions, be humble and realise we might be wrong? Can we not read more sides to an issue? (Oh, that's hard work in our fast lane *'send a text'* world.) Should we not learn from scholars and especially godly men and women as they write and share on almost every subject in the world? The generalisations about Muslims (and many other peoples) often involving prejudice and hate language should be a concern to us all. Some books are feeding the fire, and all kinds of people now claim to know so much about Islam. I may be wrong, but I see so much pride, impatience and arrogance and so little of Jesus, humility and brokenness.

It sometimes is a huge stumbling block for those who are trying to reach these different peoples with the gospel. When we meet someone we don't agree with, say on a political or doctrinal issue, are we more concerned about changing their viewpoint than we are about seeing them come to Jesus? Or if a believer, extending our love, fellowship and listening to their story? One reason some people have few friends is that they do not really love people or listen to them. They just press on in their own little world, looking down on those who are not in agreement. I guess you know this is why I wrote *The Revolution of Love* fifty years ago, alongside my other books, and why we are still pushing *The Calvary Road* by Roy Hession fifty-six years later. This is also why Charles Swindoll's *The Grace Awakening* became one of the most important books in many of our lives. The missing word with too many today is **repent** which I believe involves U-turns and change.

I believe DVDs on transformation can build faith but also total unbiblical and unrealistic expectations. It's not really new thinking. Dominion theology takes it to extreme and I believe has been discredited. History shows that it is very difficult to transform whole nations or even whole cities. A small town or village is an easier target but even there evil will be about and often outward transformation pushes people into conformity, nominal Christianity and tonnes of hypocrisy. Church history has been a favourite subject of mine for fifty-six years and backs up what I am trying to say. Maximum Salt and Light impact to me is a different story and if we bring that into our transformation theology that really helps. The tendency for charismatics and evangelicals to exaggerate is an epidemic that hurts the work of God. Of course my Messiology theology helps me stay positive in the midst of it. The idea or theory that Europe became so great because it was so-called Christian is full of holes but of course has some great elements of truth. If we want transformation, our maximum attention needs to be on our own life, then all around us and then the Church. After that, God will work in many different ways and the devil will be twice as active.

I have read many accounts of great revivals which give dreams of transformation. They did of course impact society, but are often exaggerated and don't give the full picture. Our longing for simplicity in the midst of complexity leads to just more confusion.

In the midst of the mess we see all around, even in the Church and Christian organisations, how do we press on and stay encouraged and positive? Of course there are whole books and sermons that answer this, but for me it must include Messiology, which is a different view on how God works among His people. It was hard for me as a Christian leader to admit that I had a wrong view of God and the way He works among His people. What about you?

CHAPTER 11

If You Don't Want to Get Hurt, Don't Play Rugby

I was once having lunch with Paul Dando, a pastor in Wales. He leads a live church in Narberth where I have spoken many times. I remember being there one time with my grandson Charlie who helped me on my book table. Charlie had never done this before and was surprised that we could not keep all the money people gave.

Paul shared the following story in a little restaurant in Little Haven. It was at a leaders meeting and some of the leaders were really hurting from difficulties and people in their churches. Just before an older visiting speaker from South Africa was about to bring the main message, one of them led in prayer and especially prayed for those who were hurting. The opening line of this seasoned leader's message was, *'If you don't want to get hurt, don't play rugby'*. Oh how true.

All over the world I have told people, and especially leaders, if you don't want to get hurt you're on the wrong planet. This is the way this fallen, rebellious planet is and we must learn how to press on in the midst of it. Even in the very best of healthy churches, with all our humanness, mistakes will be made. People will sin and fail and people will need help. It does not make it any easier when we think of Satan as a roaring lion seeking who he can devour. 'Be alert and of sober mind. Your enemy the devil prowls around like a roaring lion looking for someone to devour' (1 Peter 5:8).

I have been so helped and inspired by so many men and women who through every kind of hurt and difficulty have exercised forgiveness and pressed on. At the same time if we who are in leadership will live out the reality of the indwelling Holy Spirit, I believe we will personally hurt only a small number of people. I have often tried to find out if something I have said or done has hurt someone and then have gone out of the way to apologise and ask forgiveness. We need to ask ourselves how often we say sincerely, *I'm sorry, please forgive me*. Should this not be basic to our heart and vocabulary?

Misunderstandings are basic to life on this planet (I really cannot speak of other planets); I have seen thousands of them both big and small. Destructive gossip is often released not because of some clear cut sin or evil, but due to some kind of miscommunication or misunderstanding. All of our married life, Drena and I have struggled in this area. Most of the time it is a very small issue but the enemy tries to use it to bring confusion, hurt and pain. We must learn how to counter this with better listening and a greater effort to understand the person talking or the one being talked about.

The challenge to believe the best and the secular principle that a person is innocent until proven guilty is so very important. My heart has been broken when I have seen people throw these principles out of the window and just press on in their own strength.

I want to bring in here my plea to make prayer, prayer meetings or concerts (or whatever you call them) a central part of your life and ministry. One of the most important things I learned as a young Christian was how to pray and also how to make prayer meetings a top priority, which I have maintained by His grace all my life. There are hundreds of books on prayer and I don't want to repeat what others have said, but I want to remind my readers of how prayerlessness will open the door for so many setbacks, problems and hurts. I would be so encouraged to know that people have read my two chapters on this in *Drops from a Leaking Tap* and that they are putting it into practice.

This leads me to share one of the most important aspects of our walk with God, the challenge to not hold hurts or anything else against someone. By His grace I have never gone to bed with anything against people and I have been hurt and disappointed by people hundreds of times. To me it's not an option. We must forgive and even work on forgetting. The verses about loving our enemies make it even more wrong and ridiculous to hold anything against someone. To seek to get even or any form of revenge has no place in the disciple of the loving, Living Lord. This does not mean there will always be great fellowship in working together. That's often a more complex step that is not always possible. As we are more mature in our faith, and it was hard for me, we learn how to press on with unsolved relationship complexities. *How can two walk together unless they are in agreement?* That is a different level from basic love, respect and forgiveness. We have to remind ourselves often that there is only one Body. Yes, we all make up the Body of Christ.

How can we possibly think we are going to evangelise the world and plant churches among all people without every kind of problem and trial that the mind can imagine being present, including some even losing their lives for the cause of Christ? The martyrs we have had in our movement have made a huge impact on most of us and helped us get our priorities sorted out for HIS GLORY. I would urge people to read Gary Witherall's book *Total Abandon* (Tyndale House, 2005) written after the martyrdom of his wife in Lebanon. With it, please try reading R.T. Kendall's book *Total Forgiveness* (Hodder & Stoughton, 2010). For sure, serving in God's great global army is going to be tougher than rugby. Remember, 2 Timothy 2:3: 'Join with me in suffering, like a good soldier of Christ Jesus'. In fact, while you're at it, read this whole chapter.

CHAPTER 12

Moaners, Complainers, Blockers and Negative Thinkers

Wow, does this chapter title speak about you? I hope not – it's really a deadly road and too many are walking on it. I think I had some of this as a young Christian and even later on as a husband, father and Christian leader. Overall, I seem to be in many ways very optimistic, but I also have a strong negative streak. It gets more complex as God seems to use some of my negative statements, especially about the state of the Church and even the average Christian.

I recall one time in particular, we had to learn the hard way that **radical discipleship without radical GRACE is so often a hurtful, confusing dead end street**, yet God did great things in the midst of our extremism, weakness and failures. In the late 1950s and 1960s, we were on the highway of radical discipleship and were putting into practice what David Platt wrote about in *Radical*.

I remember well, being in Pakistan shortly after the work was started there about forty years ago. A door opened for a key meeting in the cathedral in a major city. Key church leaders were coming, including the Bishop of the Church of Pakistan. I was the main speaker and I remember a key OM leader asking me to be careful with what I said when I preached. I guess he knew I often said something offensive or even stupid when preaching! I guess I told him I would try my best. Then someone else asked if I could dress properly. Suits and ties were a big thing then in the Church of Pakistan and even till this day. I was never known for being well dressed but, wow, the next day I was there in suit and tie. I think I looked like an undertaker. This happened to be a time in my life when I was determined to be less negative, even in dark difficult situations. God wanted to give me a crisis to change my life for as, whilst I was speaking, a pigeon flew over me and dropped its load on my suit sleeve. What an embarrassment in front of the Bishop and all those people, many hearing me for the first time! But God was doing a new thing and I just said, 'Praise the Lord that the elephants here don't fly'. Of course there was great laughter.

Yes, you might be in a bad situation but why not thank and praise the Lord? I am sure it could be a lot worse. That does not mean you should verbally praise the Lord when someone is pouring out a hurtful, difficult situation to you. At that moment you need to remember the verse, 'Rejoice with them that do rejoice, and weep with them that weep' (Rom. 12:15, AV). At the same time we might be rejoicing in our hearts knowing God can bring something beautiful out of a terrible situation. I am reading Hanna Miley's (a wonderful former OMer) book about her life as a child coming to England on the famous trains that brought children from Germany before the Holocaust. The book is called *A Garland from Ashes* (Outskirts, 2013) and it is the story of reconciliation with those who took the lives of her parents and so many more in the concentration camps of Germany during that horrific war. There are many other similar books that we should allow God to use to change our lives.

Why are so many strong Bible-believing people (and I am one of them) so quick to criticise, often before they have the facts? Why are so many Christians moaning about so many things, especially about their governments? What do we do with Philippians 4:4–7?

> *Rejoice in the Lord always. I will say it again: rejoice!*
> *Let your gentleness be evident to all. The Lord is near.*
> *Do not be anxious about anything, but in every*
> *situation, by prayer and petition, with thanksgiving,*
> *present your requests to God. And the peace of God,*
> *which transcends all understanding, will guard your*
> *hearts and your minds in Christ Jesus.*

God does not want us to be moaning, complaining, negative, unthankful people. Please pause for a moment and allow the Holy Spirit to do a new work in your heart and life. I have spoken of this already in Chapter 2, 'Fire Extinguishers, Books and Proverbs', but want to bring out again here how this is so tied to being basically a negative person or maybe even an angry person. It was hard as a young believer to realise I had a hostility streak. I saw it come out in my speaking once and I immediately repented. It especially would come out in my driving. I found it better when I went by train.

Wherever you live today, you find people around you moaning and complaining all the time. What does it actually accomplish? To me it's very different from constructive criticism. I read a book *The Tough Minded Optimist* (Touchstone, 2003) by Dr Norman Vincent Peale, as well as other similar books, which helped change my way of thinking.

Do you spend much time with this type of person? Be sure, you will eventually become like them, it's contagious! People who always see the dark side are often actually very proud, seemingly know-it-all people, and yet that pride is often tied to insecurity which makes it an even more dangerous combination. The other day I typed out a list of things I have heard Christians moan or complain about:

> Oh, the music is too loud.
>
> Oh, they are using the wrong translation of the Bible.
>
> Oh, how can they dress like that in church?
>
> Oh, the pastor preached for too long.
>
> Oh, I wonder why his wife dresses so fancy and what she is doing with her time?
>
> Oh, Sally is so fat and Lily, she just talks so much.
>
> Oh, Sam keeps forgetting to use deodorant.
>
> Oh, did you notice the new expensive car the pastor just got?
>
> Oh, I saw one of the elders in a pub the other day.
>
> Oh dear, they had red wine in the communion glass
>
> Oh, I saw the pastor's son having a beer.

In my early days I remember Christians getting upset over women wearing lipstick or men having long hair. The list could go on. When we think and behave this way, what does it accomplish of eternal value? Do we not understand the importance of our disposition and attitude? Once again, I would urge people to read Charles Swindoll's book *The Grace Awakening*, which is now in many languages. I am reading a new book on grace called *Pharisectomy: How to Joyfully Remove Your Inner Pharisee and Other Religiously Transmitted Diseases* (Influence Resources, 2012) by Peter Haas, and you can imagine what that's about. We need to remember that God is not just concerned about what we do and say, but what we think. Attitude is a major part of our walk with Jesus.

In almost every situation, and in every person, there are positive and good things and we should focus on that much more than the negative. We also need to remember the verses 'Do not judge, or you too will be judged. For in the same way as you judge others, you will be judged' (Matt. 7:1–2).

Also, what about this great rule: 'So in everything, do to others what you would have them do to you' (Matt. 7:12). Yes, I know we are back to the message in my book *The Revolution of Love* and I hope you will embrace it with all your heart and actions. It has such a huge emphasis in the Bible. How can we miss it? Read 1 Thessalonians 5:16 and learn to 'Rejoice always'.

When it comes to being positive it's hard to beat Philippians 4:8:

> *Finally, brothers and sisters, whatever is true, whatever is noble, whatever is right, whatever is pure, whatever is lovely, whatever is admirable – if anything is excellent or praiseworthy – think about such things.*

A friend in the education world explained what a 'blocker' was as it was a new word to me. It's a person that thinks everything is fine especially with their own work and teaching and they block any effort for change. If we are to grow and be the people God wants us to be then we must keep learning and keep changing.

Complaining and criticising one's wife or husband is so often the road to a broken relationship. I, by God's grace, have seldom criticised my wife in public and not that much in private, but have had to repent of indirect statements and sometimes humour that may have sown a wrong idea about my wife to those who heard or read it. I remember once in a message paying a great tribute to my wife in more than a few sentences and then getting criticised for that as well! Have you found that sometimes life is full of no-win situations? Wow, my negative streak just popped out again. Oh, may the Lord have mercy on us all.

CHAPTER 13

Proclamation with Social Concern and Action

Can the biggest change in one's life and theology come after that person is sixty years of age? Yes, and it happened to me as well as to the movement that I helped start, Operation Mobilisation. There is only one chapter about this in *Drops from a Leaking Tap* and it's about twelve years since the big changes took place.

We need to go back to John Stott, Billy Graham and the 1974 World Congress on Evangelism in Lausanne, Switzerland where a couple of thousand Christian leaders representing the world met. I had a small seminar on the subject of 'Literature Evangelism' and I think I missed some of the key messages. There was a great debate going on about how Social Action and Proclamation fit together and in the end the famous Lausanne Document declared that they must. Many articles and books came out for and against the decision, but this Congress, plus many other people's books and movements changed the course of history. Keep in mind that some churches and missionaries were already way out front in combining these two aspects of ministry. Wow, look at General Booth and the Salvation Army. Of course, there are some lessons to learn from that as well and not all positive.

Years before this, Operation Mercy had begun under Bertil Engqvist a major leader in OM from Sweden. I remember giving the go ahead on this especially with the hope that most of the funding would come out of Sweden.

Afghanistan was one of the key nations in our vision from the very beginning and this kind of ministry was the only way to function in that nation and among the refugees over the border in Pakistan where Gordon Magney (founder of our work there and now buried in Kabul) continued with his wife Grace. They had an amazing ministry in caring for all kinds of physical needs and trying to bring the gospel at the same time. Not an easy task.

Joseph D'Souza who was the leader of the work in India was one of the pace setters of the whole movement to bring about this huge change. The Good Shepherd slum work with clinics and schools was historic in our movement and now there are over 110 much larger schools across the nation, especially for the Dalit children who are so often denied a proper education. As I have mentioned before, over 250 million in India are considered untouchable. Today they are often called Dalits. Many believe it is a form of slavery. We are not speaking of low caste people (hundreds of millions more) but of outcastes. Our concern for these people helped change the course of our history. This should not be in what is called the world's largest democracy, but it is and in God's mysterious way of working in one of the world's messiest situations, hundreds of thousands of these people are coming to Jesus.

I wrote an article that I would like to share here:

What will our grandchildren say?

Two or three generations after slavery was abolished, the grandchildren of those who believed, practised or were involved, wondered how they could have been so blind and stupid. (Choose your own words).

During my exercise walk I have been listening to Philip Yancey's book *What's So Amazing About Grace*, especially the part about segregation. We now wonder how that generation could have been so blind, racist (even professing Christians) and often hateful. To us it seems unreal.

The new generation in South Africa is amazed at what their parents believed and practised (praise Jesus for every exception) and did in those days known as Apartheid. When they watch films or read the history they find it hard to believe and often feel ashamed. Of course there was, with slavery and segregation, a remnant who defended and still defend it. Actually in parts of Europe there is a resurrection of this kind of extremism and racism. In fact a Neo-Nazi Movement is quite alive, especially in the USA.

Here is my big question to all who read this: What issues today do we have so wrong that future generations will stand in amazement at our blindness, prejudice, laziness and stupidity? Wow, now there is a finger pointing at me.

I believe it's 'UNTOUCHABILITY' that has created a group of people who are living in a form of slavery and

Apartheid with hyper-segregation. As this goes on, it affects the daily lives of over 200 million people, mainly in India but other nations as well.

Where do you stand on this issue? What are you and I doing about it? I read the papers and follow the news and could list from memory a list of a hundred famous and outstanding people in every aspect of society (where do you fit?) and hardly any one of them is doing anything about this global scourge and injustice! Let them ask what their children and grandchildren will be saying about them in the future. Let us all search our hearts.

I lived in India and missed it, but I thank God for those who helped me wake up so that one of the major goals in my life is to see this changed.

The next step for some of you may be to read Joseph D'Souza's book *Dalit Freedom: Now and Forever* (Dalit Freedom Network, 2005). We are willing to send this as a gift to anyone who sends me their address. My email is george.verwer@om.org. Please send us your address when requesting the book.

A learner still learning about Justice and Grace and a Servant of the Living God,

George Verwer

In 1998, at our annual main leaders' conference, in South Africa, I announced that I believed that in five years I should step out of the International Leadership of OM. That happened in the summer of 2003 and Peter Maiden, chosen by the Movement (quite a long process with some bumps), took over the leadership for the next ten years. It now is Lawrence Tong who is based in Singapore, where he is from.

As I was on my way out of leadership, some thought: VERWER, MR PROCLAMATION EVANGELISATION, WILL NEVER CHANGE. They got the surprise of their life as God moved me to embrace this theology of ministry. I saw it clearly in the Bible and in history. This has changed the way I think, speak and live. It especially changed how I use my time and money. Hundreds of times I have preached messages similar to the chapter about this in *Drops from a Leaking Tap*.

In our Special Project Ministry, which Peter Maiden and the leaders of OM felt I should keep and lead as part of OM, we began to get involved in more projects connected with all kinds of social concerns across the world, from the AIDS Crisis to the global impure water problem and every possible struggle connected with poverty. I realised as I moved down the road of more concern for human rights that this must include the rights of the unborn. Linked with Patrick Dixon, we flooded out a couple of hundred thousand copies of his book *AIDS Action* (Bookprint Creative, 2010) in many languages. With Randy Alcorn, we also began to flood out tens of thousands of *Why Pro-Life?: Caring for the Unborn and Their Mothers* (Hendrickson, 2012) in many languages. In some languages, it was the first Christian book on that subject ever put into print. God opened doors to share this message, even on television and radio, all over the world and through my website **www.georgeverwer.com** and other sites, the message went out far and wide.

There is not enough space in this book to go into the detail about the challenges and changes that faced us all in the movement as this took place. It has not been an easy marriage but of course marriage never is. Some felt that basic evangelism was being pushed aside and that social action projects and relief projects were totally dominating the movement.

Debates took place and papers were written. The whole work seemed to become way more complex and messy. The pressure to raise funds for all kinds of needs and crises seemed to be off the charts. Looking back, the provision of funds for so much great ministry in answer to prayer constantly amazes me. I am not sure that anyone knows how much bigger the annual budget is now in comparison to what some call the 'old days'. It has doubled a number of times. I sense we still have a good balance with every kind of evangelism. This still involves reaching millions with the gospel, which is still at the very heart of the movement and certainly in mine too. The books and audio visuals that come out of OM show that clearly. For example, in the case of my own ministry and Special Projects I speak about all these things, but since mine is a relatively small amount of money compared to OM's total income, I feel that most of it should be used for evangelistic and church planting related aspects of ministry.

I am especially encouraged with the ship ministry and the way that reaching people with the gospel is still such a top priority, especially using literature. Over 40 million have actually been up the gangway and tens of millions more have been reached in onshore outreach and church ministry.

What moved me in this direction? First of all it was a deeper study of Scripture, both the Old and New Testaments. I realised I always believed it to some degree but felt that other groups like Tearfund, World Relief and World Vision should take up that side of things. Men of God like John Stott, whose chair I am sitting in here at his special retreat cottage in the Hookses, and others of a similar mind were a huge influence. Even some with whom I did not agree caused me to search my heart and be ready for radical change.

Yes, OM has become more complicated and some don't like it and have abandoned us, but others are being raised up especially of the younger generation to carry the work forward. One of the most encouraging things in the movement is the army of younger leaders (from close to a hundred nationalities) that God has raised up to carry the vision and the work forward.

Our lives, Drena, myself and our small staff, have also become more complex. We seem to have less time to do things than we used to, like watch a film on an aeroplane. I have my own laptop screen, with hundreds of emails, and so give that priority. We have discovered a whole series of different mines and obstacles as we walk down this road, but in the end we are cast on God as we have always been. We have seen amazing answers to prayer and thanks to some great books we know more about how to handle unanswered prayer. Pete Greig, founder of the 24:7 Prayer Movement, has written a book called *God on Mute* (Regal, 2007); its front cover really ministers to me, as does Philip Yancey's *Disappointment with God* (Zondervan, 2009) and Ron Dunn's *When Heaven is Silent* (Paternoster, 1994).

CHAPTER 14

A Burden and Vision that has Never Changed

From even before my conversion I had a love for the Bible. But receiving the Gospel of John through the post in the summer of 1953, together with hearing Billy Graham's message on 3 March 1955, completely changed the course of my life.

Before this, I had attended Bible Club at Ramsey High School a few times, which might be the reason why I was sent a copy of the Gospel of John alongside the letter on the following page ...

Word of Life Camp
Schroon Lake, New York
July 15, 1953

Dear Bible Club Member:

       The summer is well started now, and I hope that you are truly enjoying it. Whether you are working or resting, I imagine that you have some spare time. As Bible Club president, I have always desired that each member read at least a portion of the Bible. During the school year, our time is quite occupied with school work, but now that you have a little time, I would like to invite you to read the portion of God's Word which is enclosed, the Gospel of John.

       There are several reasons, which I shall briefly state, why I would like you to read it. First of all the Bible itself tells you to "Search the Scriptures" in John 5:39. This is one of God's commands which we should obey. Also, there are many interesting stories in the Bible of miracles and exciting experiences which are all true, as it says in John 17:17 -- 'Thy word is truth." Also, the Bible has been a great source of enjoyment and blessing to many, including me. Only in this Book do we find God's instructions for us and our lives.

       The time spent in reading this short book would be most worthwhile and inspiring. In this short portion are included most of the basic Bible truths, and the way to find true joy, peace, and success.

       This summer will be only as worthwhile as the things which you do in it. Reading this short portion of God's Word will be very worthwhile, and I pray that it may be the source of joy and blessing. If you have any questions or problems in which I might help, please let me know. I would be most happy to help you.

       God bless you in His path.

Yours most truly,

Dannie

Daniel Clapp

Even before receiving this letter, I joined the Pocket Testament League and carried a New Testament in my pocket. I saw one of their presentations that showed their gospel preaching and distribution of John's Gospels. So the seed of wanting everyone in the world to have the Word of God was sown in my heart.

Most people know that I am involved in many aspects of God's work and also know how much I esteem all agencies and churches that are part of God's great global force. What I share now with you comes from my heart with a lot of thought from a life-time of ministry.

On my last trip to India, as I interviewed many people, I did some homework and I realised that despite all kinds of fantastic ministries, including mass evangelism, radio, TV, film shows, literature, etc, that still many hundreds of millions HAVE NEVER HEARD OR READ THE GOSPEL (including having seen a gospel film). Also, many groups have moved into holistic ministry, like the schools we have among the Dalits which involves a huge amount of time and money. Tremendous evangelism and church planting is done side-by-side and we thank the Lord for the results.

The Dalits may soon be the most reached mega-group in India, but in fact, with a population of 250 million, what percentage of them do we reach with at least something of the Message, knowing that many do not read? We are told there is somewhere around 300 million 'Other Backward Castes' (OBC), maybe more, and I wonder how many have not yet had one chance to hear or know the saving grace of Christ? This is from someone who believes that one chance to hear of Jesus is not enough.

There are over 170 million Muslims in India. Maybe if we are optimistic, many millions have been to a gospel film show, have a New Testament or Gospel or may have heard or seen a gospel radio or TV programme. What if it were even 70 million? That's 100 million to go! Do you get my point? I am not up-to-date on China, but with all the growth there no one would question that hundreds of millions have also never heard the good news.

I recently noticed huge steps forward in getting the Bible or parts of it in every language. Some of these languages represent a very small number of people; good – I believe in it. It's great to read that many extra millions of dollars are now given or pledged to this. This makes it more difficult for me to understand how there are hundreds of millions (some would say a billion) all around us whose languages we have already translated (New Testaments, tracts, DVDs, booklets, CDs etc), and yet we still have not given anything to them. **IT DOES NOT MAKE SENSE TO ME.** Maybe some of you who read this can help me out?

The claim by one group or network that we will soon lead another billion people to Jesus is, I believe, misleading but with certain parts of the world having massive church growth, who knows? I think the truth is that we will only have a small effect on the hundreds of millions who are more resistant to the gospel or live away from the areas where this response is taking place. For example, will Dalit converts in India reach Brahmans?

My plea is that we would pray more for the reaching of these unreached hundreds of millions with the message of salvation. Would you pray for the release of funds for this kind of ministry? Financial breakthroughs will enable us to give more evangelistic tools to thousands of workers who are asking for them. Ideally, money should not be the main focus, but when it is the main thing, and in my ministry it often is, then let's somehow find it! It will not be one agency or church that makes this happen, but a massive grass-roots movement (already going on) in which people even in the midst of other ministry want to reach the millions around them. We need to make every effort to teach each believer in every new church that they should be reaching out to all the lost around them – this would be a gigantic step forward.

I am going to give more time to this in my ministry and if any of you know anyone, anywhere, that has a heartbeat for this kind of thing, I would love to talk with them personally. I am thankful you have read this far and would love to hear from you.

A few years ago I decided to make a list of those ministries that have given the gospel to at least 100 million people. I called it 'The Hundred Million Club'. I can send you the list if you want, it contains about fifty agencies and ministries. Of course many people in certain nations and language groups hear and read the gospel many times. Some have a pile of gospels, tracts or booklets they have received. But hundreds of millions still have nothing.

We have much to rejoice over, but we also have so much to do.

CHAPTER 15

Where Do We Go from Here?

I am here in the beautiful home of dear friends outside one of my favourite cities, Belfast, Northern Ireland. I have been here about one hundred times, counting visits to other parts of Ireland, and it's amazing to see all that God has been doing in the midst of what I believe was one of the biggest and most horrific messes in all Europe.

All these years I have listened to criticism of the churches for not doing more about it. How easy it is to blame the Church! If the Church was so bad then why was the Living God using the Church here and saving so many people in the midst of all this? It is one of the first places in the world that gave me a wide open door to speak at one of their biggest and most important mission events. It became the most proactive part of the UK, not only for OM but dozens of other mission groups. How could God ever use someone or even a church that for example has such prejudice against the

Catholic population? This sad division in the country exists to this day and I find it a great struggle … but the Living God seems to be able to handle it. God Almighty can be grieved by people and bless people at the same time. Yes, this is what I call Messiology.

This is my final chapter and my heart and mind are so full of what I would like to share. I want to share just a little about some further issues that I would beg you to give some thought to. You may wonder why there is not more about missions and especially the unreached people in this book, but I did not want to repeat what I have written about in my other books. I am building on what I have shared in those books, hoping it will still be relevant to those who have not read them. For over ten years, the official history of OM called *Spiritual Revolution* by Ian Randall has been available, which expresses so much of what I believe and how God has worked in my life and in OM. I would urge people to read that book carefully as there is so much we can learn about how God uses all kinds of people in so many amazing ways. There also are quite a number of books about the ship ministry, including unique books like Debbie Meroff's *Psalms from the Sea* (Amazon, 2012).

I want to give a final plea for you to consider to become a career missionary. Some don't like the word missionary, so what about 'full time ambassador of Christ to the nations'? This is the decision Drena and I made before we even met and we look back at fifty-five years of work and service together. Even in her seventies, Drena is a full-time missionary working very long hours every day behind the scenes. We have had many changes but don't believe in retirement in our service of the KING. I already have a strategy for how I can stay in bed with my BlackBerry phone and laptop and carry on a good part of my work.

How sad that so many churches now have thrown away Acts 13 and no longer send out career long-term missionaries from their church. This includes good churches that I highly esteem. I am well aware of some of the negative stories circulated about missionaries (some of them are true) that cause even well-known Christian leaders to develop their false ideas. One of the most heart-breaking books written by a man I love who has been used by God urges us to stop sending cross-cultural and especially American missionaries. I guess Drena and I never should have gone to India? Do people have any idea of how many MILLIONS upon millions have come to Christ and are still coming to Christ because we have sent out missionaries? Some of those places don't need so many anymore but there are other nations, at least forty, that desperately need long-term, language-learning missionaries. I also believe in tent makers who do have jobs, but so often, in my observation, their work is all-consuming (especially if they have a family) and so there is little time left for sharing the gospel and planting a church. We rejoice over every exception.

OM has been considered to be one of the major organisations birthing short-term missions but it was not my original thinking. We, from day one, were looking for LIFERS.

We saw right away in Mexico, and much more in Europe, how wonderfully God could use short-term missions which in turn became a global phenomenon bringing hundreds of thousands into the Kingdom. Yes, lots of mistakes along the way and truly, very messy.

In all of this we learned that so often the finance was harder to find than the people. We saw great answers to prayer in connection with funds and OM was considered part of the Faith Mission Movement, which was pioneered without them knowing it by people like Hudson Taylor, C. T. Studd and many others. George Mueller, who did not outwardly ask for money, moved his whole work, mainly among orphans, by faith and prayer. He was also considered one of the founders of the Brethren Movement (one of the greatest and messiest movements in history) which, even in his lifetime, became very messy as he fell out with one of the other founders, J. N. Darby.

My own private study, shows that George Mueller was in fact, in the culture of his day, a fantastic fundraiser and I decided to follow his example. Praying and finding the finance for OM and other ministries has been one of the most exciting and motivating parts of my life. I could write a book about it but I am still praying that even better things are ahead. The New Testament clearly shows that together with prayer we need the highest level of communication, openness, honesty and integrity. We have already mentioned some books on this subject but the latest book to help me is called *Gospel Patrons* (Reclaimed Publishing, 2014) by John Rinehart. He shares his insight into how business people who have the gift and ability to make money have so often been such a vital part of what God has been doing through other anointed and gifted people.

If the message of mystery, mercy, Messiology (and grace) has not come out in this book then I have failed. Some of you who are reading this have not yet received the gift of God in salvation by believing that the Lord Jesus died for your sins. YOU need to do that now.

Others who have had this experience of new birth and grace have not forgiven themselves. This brings ongoing dysfunction and complexity into their lives and ministry. We surely have seen that God not only works in messy situations that must grieve Him at the same time, but He can work in messy people. HE WANTS TO USE YOU, no matter how many struggles and failures you have had in your life. Maybe, due to sin and folly you walk with a limp, but the main thing is that you're still walking. He may want you even walking in some other part of the world where you never expected to go. Would you at least pray about it?

Other people who are reading this have not really forgiven others, especially those who have hurt them, disappointed them or even betrayed them. Maybe they have forgiven them in the head but not in practical reality. It might be an ongoing struggle, but that step needs to be taken.

If God has spoken to you through what I have shared, I would like you to consider some other practical steps to take this message from the head down to the heart and the feet:

1. Make the decision to be more positive and optimistic and start practising by sharing some of the wonderful ways God is working locally and around the world.

2. Get involved in at least one prayer group of some kind that focuses on the nations and on the more unreached peoples. Hopefully you're involved in your local church prayer meeting but I would hope you can be involved in at least one other one. Wow, maybe you should start one?!

3. Get involved in giving out books and DVDs (or sharing websites) that have helped you and also share portions of Scripture and Christian DVDs to those who you know or meet who don't know the Lord.

4. Go on a short-term mission ASAP. Try to give preference to a ministry where you will be sharing your faith and involved with people. Try to work among the poor and live in a situation where you will be stretched.

5. Start going out of your way to meet people near you from other cultures. Start learning at least one other language. If you have already studied a language (I started Spanish even in High School), then make a decision to continue to become fluent. As soon as possible, get amongst people who have this as their first language. Choose purposely the road that seems more difficult.

6. Learn and practise using your time more productively. Less watching and more action needs to be your motto. Beware of the television trap, games trap and the endless chit-chat trap. Of course, there is room for all these things and much more (yes, even fun things), but it should only take a tiny amount of our time. Of course if you have children and grandchildren then that time has to increase. Also with friends who are not believers, we must avoid the appearance of being neurotic, extreme and uptight. Remember Paul in 1 Corinthians 9:22: 'To the weak I became weak, to win the weak. I have become all things to all people so that by all possible means I might save some.'

7. Give thought to going to Bible College. This can even be done by distance learning or extension. We have an over fifty-three-year link with Capernwray Fellowship who have short-term Bible schools in different parts of the world. One way or another you need more time in the Word of God. I especially urge people to memorise scripture which has helped transform my own life from even before my conversion. Yes, to get the Boy Scout 'God and Country Award' I had to memorise scripture. Romans 8 was the chapter. Wow, the other day I saw a photo of my being given this award.

8. Make the decision and practise being more thankful daily. Has anyone given you anything lately? Even a book, a cup of tea or a ride to the station? Have you thanked them? I do have a friend who seems to thank people too much. I think he might be the only one? I give lots of books away. Most people never thank me unless of course I personally hand it to them and then generally there is that automatic personal thank you, but to later get any kind of thank you letter on even a tiny note would be a surprise. I thank Jesus that He has forgiven me for the times I have not been thankful or not thanked people properly with love.

9. Work harder at getting good sleep, eating the right food and a good amount of exercise. This has been my lifelong practice and I really recommend it. One of the most powerful verses in the New Testament for me is 1 Corinthians 9:24–27:

Do you not know that in a race all the runners run,
but only one gets the prize? Run in such a way as to
get the prize. Everyone who competes in the games
goes into strict training. They do it to get a crown
that will not last; but we do it to get a crown that
will last for ever. Therefore I do not run like someone
running aimlessly; I do not fight like a boxer beating
the air. No, I strike a blow to my body and make it
my slave so that after I have preached to others, I
myself will not be disqualified for the prize.

10. Make a decision to keep in touch with more people, mixing it in with prayer where you can. Use a good variety of methods but remember face-to-face over a coffee, tea or water is the best. Going out together in loving, serving and reaching others might be even better. I love email and Facebook but my telephoning quota has dropped and I realised that there is something extra special in hearing a person's voice. Wow, Praise the Lord for Skype and other similar ways of conversation. This must be mixed with forgiveness as people may let you down or you might feel some rejection in it all. The great mistake is to fail to take the initiative. I am in touch with many people who need money and I have a fund for just such people (called Special Projects) but guess why so many never get any money? THEY NEVER ask. By the way, there are fantastic books on how to raise funds and I have been blessed by them, especially *Funding the Family Business* (Stewardship, 2006) by Myles Wilson and *Friend Raising* (YWAM, 2012) by Betty Barnett.

11. Try to get some kind of mentoring and accountability even if it seems imperfect and spasmodic. If you are married, make sure you are getting enough time with your wife and family. Don't expect that to be easy. All of our lives, Drena and I have struggled especially in praying more together. And remember, if you have serious struggles with lust or pornography, YOU really need to get some help.

If you have finished reading my book, then I would love to get an e-mail from you letting me know what God has been doing in your life. It would also be a help to know if you have read any of my other books: *The Revolution of Love, Literature Evangelism, Hunger for Reality* (originally *Come! Live! Die!*), *No Turning Back* (Paternoster, 2008) and *Drops from a Leaking Tap*. It is hard to believe that the total distribution has gone over 1,000,000 copies in about fifty languages. Praise the Lord.

For me, finishing this book has been a long marathon but I see the finishing tape ahead and I am thankful for all the HELP from Above along the way. I am thankful for all the wonderful people of God who influenced my life these seventy-seven years and I just humble myself before the Lord in thanksgiving and worship.

Recommended Reading

Alexander Strauch, *If You Bite and Devour One Another*
(Lewis and Roth, 2011)

Alexander Strauch, *Leading with Love* (Lewis and Roth, 2006)

Andrew Murray, *Humility* (CreateSpace, 2012)

Betty Barnett, *Friend Raising* (YWAM, 2012)

Billy Graham, *Freedom From The Seven Deadly Sins* (Zondervan, 1963)

Billy Graham, *Peace with God* (Thomas Nelson, 2000)

Billy Graham, *The Secret of Happiness* (Thomas Nelson, 2002)

Brennan Manning, *The Ragamuffin Gospel* (Multnomah, 2005)

Charles Swindoll, *The Grace Awakening* (Thomas Nelson, 2006)

Chris Wright (ed.), *John Stott: A Portrait by His Friends* (IVP, 2011)

Chua Wee Hian, *Learning to Lead* (Authentic India, 2010)

David Platt, *Radical* (Random House, 2010)

Debbie Meroff, *Psalms from the Sea* (Amazon, 2012)

Elaine Rhoton, *The Doulos Story* (BookRix, 2014)

Elaine Rhoton, *The Logos Story* (Paternoster, 1992)

Elisabeth Elliot, *Through Gates of Splendour* (Authentic Media, 2005)

Gary Witherall, *Total Abandon* (Tyndale House, 2005)

Gordon MacDonald, *Ordering Your Private World* (Thomas Nelson, 2012)

Gordon MacDonald, *Rebuilding Your Broken World* (Thomas Nelson, 2004)

Hanna Zack Miley, *A Garland from Ashes* (Outskirts, 2013)

Hoise Birks, *A New Man* (H B Publishing, 2012)

Ian Randall, *Spiritual Revolution* (Authentic Media, 2008)

J. David Lundy, *Servant Leadership for Slow Learners* (Paternoster, 2002)

J. Oswald Sanders, *Spiritual Leadership* (Moody, 2007)

John Rinehart, *Gospel Patrons* (Reclaimed Publishing, 2014)

John Stott, *Basic Christianity* (IVP, 2012)

Joseph D'Souza, *Dalit Freedom: Now and Forever*
(Dalit Freedom Network, 2005)

Myles Wilson, *Funding the Family Business* (Stewardship, 2006)

Noah (film), directed by Darren Aronofsky (2014)

Norman Vincent Peale, *The Tough Minded Optimist* (Touchstone, 2003)

Oswald Smith, *The Passion for Souls* (Welch, 1986)

Patrick Dixon, *AIDS Action* (Bookprint Creative, 2010)

Peter Greig, *God on Mute* (Regal, 2007)

Peter Haas, *Pharisectomy: How to Joyfully Remove Your Inner Pharisee and Other Religiously Transmitted Diseases* (Influence Resources, 2012)

Philip Yancey, *Disappointment with God* (Zondervan, 2009)

Philip Yancey, *What's So Amazing About Grace?* (Zondervan, 2002)

Quo Vadis (film), directed by Mervyn LeRoy (1951)

R.T. Kendall, *Holy Fire* (Charisma House, 2014)

R.T. Kendall, *Total Forgiveness* (Hodder & Stoughton, 2010)

Randy Alcorn, *The Grace and Truth Paradox* (Multnomah, 2003)

Randy Alcorn, *Why Pro-Life?: Caring for the Unborn and Their Mothers* (Hendrickson, 2012)

Rodney Hui and George Simpson, *Logos HOPE* (BookRix, 2014)

Ron Dunn, *When Heaven is Silent* (Paternoster, 1994)

Roy Hession, *The Calvary Road* (CLC, 1980)

Theodore Epp, *Love is the Answer* (Back to the Bible, 1960)

Tom Hovestol, *Extreme Righteousness* (Moody, 1997)

Viv Thomas, *Second Choice* (Paternoster, 2000)

William MacDonald, *True Discipleship* (Gospel Folio, 2003)

Other works by George Verwer

In order of reference:

Hunger for Reality (Authentic Lifestyle, 1996) – originally entitled *Come! Live! Die!*

Drops from a Leaking Tap (Authentic Media, 2011)

Out of the Comfort Zone (Bethany House, 2000)

'Grace Awakened Leadership' – a booklet which combines the chapters on 'Grace' and 'Leadership' from *Out of the Comfort Zone* (Bethany House, 2000)

The Revolution of Love (Authentic Media, 2008)

Book by Book: Proverbs DVD (Biblical Frameworks, 2015)

Book by Book: Proverbs Study Guide, written by Paul Blackham (Biblical Frameworks, 2015)

George – for real DVD (CWR, 2015)

Literature Evangelism (Authentic Lifestyle, republished in 2003) – George's first book

No Turning Back (Paternoster, 2008)

George – for real (DVD)

Follow George Verwer on his travels to India, Mexico, Hong Kong, the UK, and his home city of New Jersey and discover that God's grace has no restrictions. This fly-on-the-wall documentary captures the energy, enthusiasm, vision and humanity of one man's life and mission. Founder of Operation Mobilisation, George's story inspires, challenges and encourages those who wonder if God can ever use them for His glory.

DVD – Approx. 55 minutes
EAN: 5027957-001602

For current prices visit **www.cwr.org.uk/store**
Available online or from Christian bookshops.

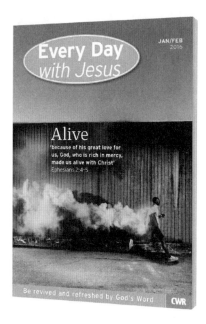

Every Day with Jesus

With around half a million readers, this bimonthly devotional is one of the most popular daily Bible reading notes in the world.

- Get practical help with life's challenges
- Gain insight into the deeper truths of Scripture
- Be challenged, comforted and encouraged
- Study six topics in depth each year
- Get more out of each issue with free online extras for groups, including discussion starters.

Available as individual issues or annual subscriptions, in large print, daily email or eBook/Kindle formats.

For current prices visit **www.cwr.org.uk/store**

Available online or from Christian bookshops.

Courses and seminars

Publishing and media

Waverley Abbey College

Conference facilities

Transforming lives

CWR's vision is to enable people to experience personal transformation through applying God's Word to their lives and relationships.

Our Bible-based training and resources help people around the world to:
• Grow in their walk with God
• Understand and apply Scripture to their lives
• Resource themselves and their church
• Develop pastoral care and counselling skills
• Train for leadership
• Strengthen relationships, marriage and family life and much more.

Our insightful writers provide daily Bible reading notes and other resources for all ages, and our experienced course designers and presenters have gained an international reputation for excellence and effectiveness.

CWR's Training and Conference Centres in Surrey and East Sussex, England, provide excellent facilities in idyllic settings – ideal for both learning and spiritual refreshment.

CWR Applying God's Word
to everyday life and relationships

CWR, Waverley Abbey House,
Waverley Lane, Farnham,
Surrey GU9 8EP, UK

Telephone: **+44 (0)1252 784700**
Email: **info@cwr.org.uk**
Website: **www.cwr.org.uk**

Registered Charity No. 294387
Company Registration No. 1990308